Independency & Presbyterianism:

REVIEW OF THE CONTROVERSY

BETWEEN THE

REV. MESSRS. CARLILE AND MORGAN,

&c.

By PHILALETHES.

"In the conflict of opposite principles, it is better openly to argue the merits of the question, than, *by indirect or concealed means to injure the character*, or the *interests* of those of another persuasion. The malignant adversary is often, to appearance, the most *placid* and *silent*; while men who enter into controversy with warmth and perseverance, give no less frequently the most convincing evidence that, instead of violating, they are honestly obeying the *law of love*."—
GREVILLE EWING.

DUBLIN:
JOHN ROBERTSON AND CO.
MDCCCXXXIV.

ADVERTISEMENT.

To those acquainted with the controversy between the Rev. J. CARLILE and the Rev. J. MORGAN, as the conductor of the *Orthodox Presbyterian*, it is unnecessary to say that the former has been most unkindly treated. There was nothing whatever personal, censorious, or unchristian, in his first publication. What, then, could have induced *Mr. Morgan*—("Who would not grieve if Atticus were he?") to assail the character of his friend, and that of the Church over which he presides, with such bitterness? Some have attributed it to an infirmity of temper, arising, perhaps, from indisposition; and they hoped that his subsequent conduct would, in some measure, undo an act so unworthy of his character. But, as if he were resolved to deprive even friendship of every excuse she could plead in his favour, he comes forward again and again (not *openly*—that would have been manly and honourable—but anonymously), heaping insult upon insult.

Mr. Carlile's reply to the "Review" is so completely triumphant, so utterly unassailable by legitimate argumentation, and yet so free from the acrimonious spirit of his opponents, that Mr. Morgan seems to have "given it up" in despair. But "a Student" has chivalrously come forward, and flung down his gauntlet. This gentleman has discovered so much littleness of mind, a spirit so coarse, and a want of courtesy so unusual, that Mr. Carlile would not condescend to notice *him*. As, however, his article has been lauded by Mr. Morgan, and circulated industriously in a separate form, I felt called on to examine it. Mr. Morgan is well known to be the writer of the "review." I need not, therefore, apologize for my title page: it is a "faithful index."

One word about Mr. Carlile's alleged ignorance of the Greek alphabet. Did it not occur to these critics that there *might* have been an *error of the press?* Would not charity, "which thinketh no evil," have suggested the possibility, at least, of such a thing? Now what are the facts of the case, as I have learned by inquiry? Mr. Carlile quoted from his own Greek Testament (Wetstein's), and being obliged to go out of town, he left it with the printers, in order to correct the press; and they, not noticing the distinction between σ and ς, or between this latter and the compound $\sigma\tau$, committed the mistake which has been so greedily seized on to injure Mr. Carlile's literary character. Was a quotation from Scripture ever called a plagiarism before? The "Student" slanderously insinuates, that the Independent Ministers are uneducated. Let him beware. "Comparisons are odious." We are not afraid to make them, and we have materials at hand. But we do not wish to be driven to a task so invidious, and so little calculated to edify the public.

The writer is altogether unacquainted with his opponents. His good-humoured raillery need not, therefore, be mistaken for personality. He is disposed to make all reasonable allowance for prejudice, and even bigotry in good men; but he cannot allow Truth to be mangled with impunity, nor suffer impertinence to pass unrebuked.

Belfast, April 1, 1834.

INDEPENDENCY AND PRESBYTERIANISM.

It is not at all desirable that two christian communities, agreeing in essentials, should be engaged in controversy about matters of minor importance, when the common enemy is at the gates, and they should combine all their energies to repel his attacks. His policy is to divide and rule—to sow dissensions in the camp, and thereby weaken the cause of Christ. If it be possible, we should live peaceably with all men, especially with the followers of the Lamb. But occasions sometimes arise, when no alternative is left us but the betrayal and sacrifice of truth, or the disruption of the social tie. If the real or pretended soldiers of Christ plead for the admission of his enemies into the garrison, we are compelled to withstand them face to face, whatever it may cost us. It is our duty to point out every departure from the truth—every aggression on christian liberty—and every abuse that may open up a source of defilement to the church, even though we should be assailed with a shower of curses, and branded as radicals and schismatics. What is the history of Highchurchism in every age, but an incessant struggle with the spirit of reformation, whenever it made its appearance, and the most strenuous efforts, open or insidious, to extinguish freedom of inquiry, and trample on the rights of conscience? So long as the apostles of error continue to disseminate their poison, and the armies of intolerance go forth to coerce the conscientious, the man of God dares not decline the work of controversy, however painful to his feelings. He may exclaim with the prophet—"Woe is me, my mother, that thou hast borne me a man of strife and a man of contention to the whole earth;" but he must not shrink from the task of contending earnestly for the faith once delivered to the saints. His duty consists not in throwing down the Sword of the Spirit for the sake of peace; but in seeking, while he wields it, to have his heart more and more imbued with the love of Christ.

Such was the disposition in which Mr. Carlile commenced this discussion, and in this spirit he has continued to conduct it. Whether those who have undertaken to canvass his reasonings have manifested a similar temper, the public will judge. Indeed, I believe they have already decided that the treatment he has received is far from christian. We wish not to retort invidious comparison and angry personality: we will not return railing for railing. Our business is to reason calmly from the Scriptures, and not to stir up the *odium theologicum* of our party.

It is generally known that the Rev. JAMES MORGAN is the writer of a review of Mr. Carlile's pamphlet in the *Orthodox Presbyterian*. This review betrayed a soreness of feeling, and an acerbity of temper, that greatly surprised all that were acquainted with the amiable character of its author; and certainly it seems difficult to account for the spirit in which it is written. Mr. Carlile published a reply to the arguments, without noticing the personalities of his opponent. And though, according to the tactics of controversy, he affected to despise this calm and argumentative production, it is manifest, it told with no small effect; for Mr. Morgan became still more angry; and feeling, it would seem, his powers unequal to the contest, he retired from the field, having engaged "a student" to come forward in his place. Accordingly, this "young" hero advances with haughty strides, and brandishes his controversial club, to the great terror of his majesty's subjects.

With this spectral Goliah, however, this "shadow of a shade," Mr. C. would, of course, feel it degrading to enter the lists. If Mr. Morgan were as eager to mantain the cause of truth, as, *it is to be feared*, he is to injure the character and interests of his opponent, he would doubtless come forward in *propria persona*, and openly maintain his principles, instead of sending forth his poisoned arrows from a masked battery. Whenever he finds it prudent to do so, I believe Mr. Carlile will be ready to examine his "reasons."

I have carefully read, again and again, what the "Student" has written in reply to Mr. Carlile on the COMPULSORY SUPPORT of RELIGION, and I must confess I cannot understand it. It may be very convincing, for aught I know; but it is above my comprehension. This young theological Quixote has a very confused way of expressing himself. I wish some of his tutors would give him a lecture on perspicuity, or at least keep him from "rushing into print," till he has got a greater command of the English language; (he lets us know himself he is a great Greek scholar,)—for manifestly his knowledge of his mother tongue "is so indefinite and scanty," that he labours under a lamentable lack of words to convey his ideas, or he knows not how to use those he has.

Mr. Carlile's argument was very intelligible; it was this—If all the members of a commonwealth are equally loyal, and contribute equally their just proportion in sustaining the national burdens, and supplying the public purse, then out of this purse, to endow one or more sects, to the exclusion of the rest, is a violation of political equity. It is *pampering* one party, and *degrading* the rest, without any just cause whatever for doing either. This is simple enough. But suppose the state anxious to avoid this injustice, and yet willing to support religion by taxation—what is to be done? Just what Mr. Carlile says—Fundamental *truth* and fundamental *error* will receive equal encouragement from the throne. Indeed it is so at present, to a great extent; for Popery, Prelacy, and Presbyterianism, bow down at his Majesty's footstool together, each holding up her hand for the pension.

In reply to this plain statement of the case, which Mr. Carlile by a familiar illustration, placed in the most convincing point of view, the "Student" treats us to a tirade of nonsense, which he calls logic, and which he has endeavoured to render still more mystical and formidable by a number of triple notes of admiration!—How much like a school boy—how *puerile!*

The confusion in his mind seems to be occasioned by mixing up things temporal with things spiritual—things that relate to man, as a *member of society*, with things that relate to him as a *subject of the King of kings*. The *former* fall under the civil magistrate's jurisdiction; with the *latter* he has, or, at least, ought to have, no concern; they lie beyond his province as a magistrate. If this obvious distinction be kept in mind, it will explain the apparent inconsistency of those who oppose establishments, and yet defend Sabbath Legislation and National Education. It is *only* as *both* questions have a bearing on the *temporal interests* of man, that the civil power is warranted to interfere.

Thus the "Student's" smoky logic, his "sound and fury" —all signify nothing. This young gentleman's mind is full of Aristotle and the old divines, and he treats us to various morceaux of logic, and metaphysical theology. He tells us of "abstract terms" and "concrete"—of "genera" and "species," and a world of learned things, with which, being no doubt, a diligent student in his way, his mind is stuffed to repletion. If, however, he could take time to digest his abstractions and concretions, and try to bring a portion of common sense, and some modesty, to the examination of these questions, he would deserve more respect. But

"A little learning is a dangerous thing."

He is manifestly a "novice;" and stimulated by the characteristic propensity of such persons, he is panting for glory on the field of controversy. According to custom, in such cases, he supplies his lack of argument with low minded ribaldry, childish sophistry, and contemptible logomachy. We wish the Editor of the Orthodox Presbyterian joy of such a champion, and we do not envy him the honourable post of *trumpeter* on this interesting occasion. Is the cause so desperate, that it must be abandoned to such advocacy?

As Mr. Carlile's triumphant exposure of the political injustice and the unchristian character of a state support for religion, remains unaffected by anything that has appeared on the other side, we shall proceed to examine the ELDERSHIP. But here we are interrupted by the "*Student*."

"When and where," quoth he in a fury, "have Presbyterians adopted and sanctioned the use of the term *lay*-elder." Answer, In an Appendix to a Sermon preached on the 26th of June, 1832, and published same year, by the Rev. James Morgan, Minister of the Presbyterian Church, &c. &c. But what meaneth this blustering? Are ruling elders *not* laymen? Are they clergymen? If neither laity nor clergy, *what* are they? Truly this is an extraordinary *species* of beings! If not a *lusus naturæ*, it is certainly a *lusus ecclesiæ*—one of those non-descript productions of mother church, which ecclesiastical naturalists have been unable to reduce to either of the two grand classes, into which they have divided the inhabitants of Christendom.

It will be admitted by our opponents, that in ascertaining the nature of an office in the church, we should not depend on one or two, or any number of *ambiguous expressions*, which, though they may come in to corroborate plainer texts, cannot by themselves be received in evidence, because they cannot teach anything *decisive*. Now, the passages* that have been quoted in support of the eldership, are *all* of this class. If there could be any decisive evidence brought forward from another quarter, they might confirm it; but of themselves they can prove nothing.

On Romans xii. 6–8, Mr. Morgan has the following remarks, in Appendix to his Sermon above mentioned. "The principle *seems* to be assumed, that there is in every church, duly constituted, an order of men, whose *exclusive business* is that of ruling." Mr. Morgan is too good a critic to maintain that this principle is distinctly *asserted*. It is only "assumed." And even in this, the writer is not confident: it only *seems* to be assumed. Thus he virtually abandons the stronghold of the eldership. But will he maintain that there is here any reference to church officers at all, as distinct from others? It appears to me, that the Apostle is exhorting believers *universally*, to avail themselves of every opportunity of doing good, each according to his ability—"according to the grace that is given" to him; not as office-bearers, exclusively, but, as sustaining *any* relation, whatever, either to the church or to society at large. There is no more *special* or *exclusive* reference in these verses, to officers of the church, than in those which follow them to the end of the chapter. Besides, if there be an authority here for one distinct ecclesiastical office, there is an equally decisive authority for *seven* distinct ecclesiastical offices. Why are the exhorter, the distributer, the dispenser of mercy, &c., expunged from the list as nonofficial? If you say, they may be included in the *ruler*, we say, with better reason, the ruler may be included in the *exhorter*. The only assumption here, in reference to ruling, is, that believers were called to the exercise of authority in various relations of life, and they are exhorted to attend to it with diligence, whether as pastors, parents, masters, stewards, &c. As to the *specific nature* of the authority, there is nothing said, or so much as hinted.

Equally futile will be found the attempt to establish the authority of the ruling elder from 1 Cor. xii. 28. It is true, there is an allusion to government in the church. "Order is heaven's first law;" and if it exist anywhere, we may expect to see it reigning in Zion, the city of our God. But the ques-

---

* Rom. xii. 6—8. 1 Cor. xii. 28. 1 Tim. v. 17. Acts xiv. 23. Titus, i. 5.

tion is not whether the church be *governed;* but, whether the governing power rests with a set of men whose "exclusive business" is to rule? This is the point at issue; and on this point the passage is totally silent. Alas, how weak is the human mind! "Trifles light as air become confirmation strong" in the hands of a thorough-paced advocate of the "religion of his fathers." Prejudice is a kaleidescope that exhibits, in proportions most beautiful, and colours most fascinaing, the ugliest monster that was ever engendered by error, or nursed by self-interest.

Dr. Campbell's argument on the word μαλιστα, "especially," has never yet been answered. Mr. Carlile has shown most conclusively, that if Dr. M'Leod's view of the passage be correct, the *practice* of the Presbyterian Church is unscriptural; for they do not pay the lay elders as they are commanded. "*Let* those that rule well be counted worthy of double honour"—that is, a competent support. This argument Mr. Morgan could not answer, and therefore he calls it "puerile,"—a very convenient way of getting over a difficulty, truly! But I fancy it will not satisfy the judicious.

In reading this much litigated passage, the stress should be laid on "labour." The phrase "in word and doctrine" will then be found in some degree explanatory of "rule." For how is the ruling performed? Is it not by diligently enforcing the Word of God? The verb κοπιαω strictly means to *toil*, to *labour hard.* Thus in Matt. vi. 28, we read—the lilies *toil* not (οὐ κοπιᾷ); and the same word is employed in Luke v. 5, where Peter says "we have *toiled* (κοπιασαντες) all night, and have taken nothing." It is also used John iv. 6, to express great fatigue. "Jesus, therefore, *being wearied,* (κεκοπιακως) sat thus on the well." From these examples, then, it is clear, that the words may be paraphrased thus—"Let those pastors that rule well, especially those that are *anxiously laborious, pains-taking, devoted* in word and doctrine, be counted worthy of an honourable maintenance."

The following familiar illustration may serve to render the point still clearer—"Let servants be counted worthy of their wages, especially the diligent and faithful." Does this imply that only the diligent and faithful are to receive wages, and that these latter constitute a class essentially distinct from servants in general, as the species is distinct from the genus?— Yet such is the logic of our opponents. According to them, "the diligent and faithful" should mean stewards, or gardeners, or masons, or the regular professors of some peculiar craft. Alas! for such logic!

I beg to bring forward another illustration, which the conduct of Mr. Carlile's opponents has perhaps suggested already to the reader. "Let critics that write poorly have their reward, especially such as labour in detraction and misrepresentation." Does this language imply that the calumnious and malignant critic constitutes a distinct *species* of the critical tribe? Is not all the distinction *personal*, and does it not consist solely in the *animus* by which he is actuated? Just so is it with the elders of the New Testament.

It is idle to quote Acts xiv. 23, and Tit. i. 5, in this controversy. They prove a plurality of elders in some churches; but they hint nothing to show that they were *not all* preachers, and are therefore totally irrelevant. Let Scripture interpret Scripture. Examine those passages that speak distinctly and formally of the standing officers of the church—that point out their qualifications and their duties. Among such passages, is there a single word of *ruling* officers in the church, distinct from those who teach? Not one! They may stretch the Bible on the rack of tortuous criticism; but it is still silent. They cannot extort from it one solitary admission in their favour.

Teaching, feeding, exhorting, edifying, and various other employments, indicative of the functions of the bishop or pastor, are mentioned in scripture, *in connexion with ruling*. But ruling itself is pointed to, as *a distinct* and *separate* office —*never*. Even Dr. Whitby admits that the elders at Ephesus were all *bishops*; and the Apostle exhorts them to "*feed*" the church of God—Acts xx. 28. When Paul gives directions, Titus, i. 5-9, about ordaining *elders*, he calls these very elders bishops, although there was a *plurality* of them in the *same* church. "For a *bishop* must be blameless," &c. And were they not all preachers? Yes; for they must be "able by *sound doctrine* both *to exhort and convince* gainsayers;" they must be "apt to teach."

The "Student" contends, that according to our interpretation of this passage, every bishop should have a *wife*. Is he serious? So it would seem: for he attempts to "render a reason," which is this—If the Apostle means only to condemn polygamy, then it would follow that all except bishops might have a plurality of wives. "Admirable critic!" Why, if this be legitimate criticism, we may demonstrate from this very passage, that every man who has not the good fortune to be a bishop, *may be* riotous, unruly, disreputable, self-willed, irrascible, a drunkard, a striker, and a slave of filthy lucre! And this is the yonng man that presumes to read lectures to Mr. Carlile on the principles of the English language! O shame, whither art thou fled? If thou hast ceased to diffuse thy hectic over the pale visage of the college-pent student, where shall we find thee?

This admirable " Student" is fond of the *dilemma.* " How soft your horn is," exclaimed the simpleton, when he seized a donkey by the ear. The " Student's" dilemmas, doubtless have *horns,* but like *aures asini,* they are very soft, and very harmless. His logic is as pointless as his insolence is contemptible. But I have done with him.

We return to our argument. Peter as well as Paul exhorts the elders without distinction to "feed the flock of God, *exercising the episcopal office,* (επισκοπουντες) not by constraint, but willingly—not for filthy lucre, but of a ready mind." —1 Peter, v. 2. From these passages, it is perfectly evident that the office of *all* the elders was episcopal or pastoral; and also, that a competent salary was, even then, allotted to the minister. If not, why should the office be coveted from love of " filthy lucre?"

It appears to the writer after long and patient inquiry, that a Congregational Church, planted in a heathen land, to which two or more ministers dispense the word of life, extending at the same time, their missionary labours, as far as possible round the country; while the more aged partor assists the younger by his counsel and experience, presiding, of course, at their meetings, but never presuming to dictate or command; and the deacons, too, as well as the members of the church, contributing according to their ability—to their mutual edification, and the diffusion of truth in the world, but altogether independent, as a church, on foreign authority or control; presents the *nearest* resemblance to the primitive model of a christian church that can be found in modern times. This view of the subject is fully justified by the impartial testimony of Ecclesiastical History, which yields not the slightest countenance to the figment of the lay eldership. But of this, more hereafter. We proceed now to consider

CHURCH AUTHORITY.

Whether, upon the whole, the power assumed by ecclesiastics, has been a blessing or a curse to the world, may be a a matter of dispute. In the days of the Goths and Vandals, it may, in some instances, have been employed with advantage to

"Curb the wild fury of a barbarous age;"

but there cannot be a question, that in more recent times, it has been invariably exerted to resist the spirit of reformation—to crush the liberties of the people, and to sustain the unrighteous domination of the most iniquitous despots that ever lived.

It is indeed a deep-rooted and wide-spreading upas, which distils barrenness and death, blighting every plant of liberty that may happen to spring up beneath its destructive shade. Thank God, its largest branches are lopped off. Like the idol, Dagon, it is mutilated, and only the "stump remains." But the stump would sprout again; and therefore we shall continue to apply the axe to the root, till not a fibre of it remains to curse the earth.

But it is said, that we have gone to another extreme, and we are insultingly told that the "Independent minister is often the best ruled man in the assembly." This is a stale joke; but bigotry is voracious, and has strong powers of digestion. Mr. Carlile has produced a mass of evidence on the subject of deacons and ruling elders, which Mr. Morgan, and all the friends he can summon to his assistance, will find it utterly impossible to answer. They have not touched it: it remains still in its integrity, to baffle their efforts and to vex their spirits. His reasoning on ecclesiastical courts is equally triumphant—equally irresistible. Let the reader consult it again; and although he may not go the full length with the writer, yet will he be constrained to admit that the two attempted replies that have been published are *utter failures*.

Mr. Carlile has shown that the authority of christian ministers cannot be *legislative;* that it consists merely in expounding and applying the laws of Christ. But the "Student," whom I find myself obliged to notice again, though I do it with reluctance, contends, on behalf of Presbyterian ministers, for a higher authority than this. "Executive authority," he says, "is no authority." Indeed! Then the authority of the parent, the master, the magistrate, the high sheriff, the Lord Lieutenant of Ireland, or even of the King, in his executive capacity, is no authority. I should suppose this student aspires to the chair of moral philosophy. He seems destined to make some notable discoveries in the science of ethics. Will he not be at issue with his tutor on this subject? Has not *he* authority over his class to enforce the standing laws of the college. Let the " Student" be cautious: he may be made to *feel* that there is such a thing as *executive* authority. I hope his conduct will never disgrace the college; but should it be found grossly improper, there would be no need, I suppose, to obtain an act of parliament for his expulsion.

What then? Is the authority of christian ministers an authority to *make laws to bind the consciences of men?* Does the Synod of Ulster claim *this* authority? If so, they are symbolizing with popery more thoroughly than might have been expected from the followers of Knox and Calvin. Was it to vindicate this authority that the covenanting confessors of Scotland suffered themselves to be immolated on the bloody altars of popery and prelacy? Could this "Student" be a Jesuit in disguise? Let Mr. Morgan look to it, that he be not imposed on. In reading the history of the illustrious fathers of the Scottish Church, the members of the Synod of Ulster may well exclaim,

" Tempora mutantur et nos mutamur in illis."

But certainly they are not so very bad as their young advocate has made them appear. Doubtless, some of them are convinced, ere now, that he has more zeal than discretion, and more logic than wisdom. Logic is a sharp tool, which he knows not well how to manage; and in attempting to wound Mr. Carlile, the poor young gentleman has cut his own fingers sadly. But it is by such painful experiments that we learn prudence.

What is the nature and extent of the authority claimed for Presbyterian ministers in their own authorized standard, the *Code of Discipline?* We shall see. "The power possessed by teachers of the church amounts to not more than this: To search the mind of the Spirit speaking in the Scriptures, to produce *Scripture authority* for the truth of what they teach; and to practise those rites, and those *only*, which *Christ* has sanctioned by his *example*, prescribed by his *authority*, and recorded in his word." Is this *legislative* authority? Is this any other authority than that which Independent Ministers claim and exercise?

Again—"In exercising the *unalienable right* of *his own judgment*" the believer, "refuses to acknowledge subjection of conscience to *any authority* but the WORD OF GOD." Again, it is said, the church member must be "thoroughly persuaded in his own mind" by a personal examination of the Scriptures, before he receives as truth any statement which his pastor may advance.—*Code of Discipline*, p. 10.

Where now is the warrant for claiming legislative authority for Presbyterian ministers? None whatever is to be found in their standards. Shall we say, then, that they have, as pastors, properly, no authority? Let Mr. Morgan settle that question with the "Student," and the Session, and the Managing Committees; but in order to help him to a satisfactory conclusion, I shall furnish him with another law from the Code of Discipline:—"The minister shall not issue *any point of discipline by his own authority;* nor shall he have a *negative voice against the decision of the majority*"—p. 17.

Now, were we as eager to irritate the feelings, as we are anxious to enlighten the mind and convince the judgment, we might, after reading such passages as these, say that the Presbyterian minister is fettered and manacled, so that he cannot stir a step without permission of the *oligarchy* by which his movements are controlled—that he is "the best ruled man in the congregation"—that, in a word, he is but a cat's paw in the hands of the Session. But instead of imitating our brethren in conduct like this, we go on patiently and meekly, endeavouring to instruct them from the Bible and their own authorized standards; showing that the authority exercised by Congregational Ministers is the *only legitimate* authority—the only authority that can be justified by Scripture, or maintained without violating the rights of conscience; and though our brethren frequently abuse us for the pains we take with them in these particulars, yet still we say, "Strike, but hear!"

If, after all, they claim a right to *legislate* for the church, and to lord it over God's heritage, we can only say, with the patriarch—"O my soul, come not thou into their secret; unto their assembly, mine honour, be not thou united!"

In regard to the assumed representative character of the assembly at Jerusalem, whose proceedings are recorded in the 15th of Acts, Mr. Carlile according to the laws of controversy, threw the *onus* of proof on his opponents. And we have seen the Reviewer's "young" friend groaning and panting beneath his burden, in a manner calculated to excite the compassion of the most hard-hearted spectator. He reiterates again and again the μυριαδες of Dr. M'Leod, and with still greater bluster than the doughty Doctor, he demands what house could be large enough to contain these myriads, these tens of thousands?

In a similar tone and spirit the infidel demands how a country so small and sterile as Palestine could support the vast population which the Scriptures ascribe to that country; and without waiting for an answer, he exclaims with vehemence, " the Bible is an imposture!" Of course, we must leave the man to enjoy his triumph. So, when the Presbyterian has reckoned the "myriads" that were converted at Jerusalem, he thinks he has refuted Independency; and having jumped to this conclusion with the agility of passion, rather than arrived at it by the more tedious and painful process that reason would point out, he refuses to hear a word more on the subject. We cannot help such a man: let him enjoy his fancied triumph. But to the more rational portion of our readers, we would submit the following considerations:—

That the numbers of the believers at Jerusalem "did not prevent their meeting together in *one place*, we have direct evidence; for where their numbers are mentioned, *their meeting together in one place is also mentioned*." Acts ii. 41–47; v. 12; xxi. 20–22.

Besides, "in estimating their numbers, we must make large allowance for *death* and *dispersion*," and we may add for *defection* also; for it is reasonable to suppose that many persons, struck with admiration and awe at the miraculous powers that were exhibited, " believed," and submitted to baptism just as Simon Magus did; but not having the root of the matter, remained in the gall of bitterness, and the bond of iniquity. This diminution of numbers " would take place especially in the city of Jerusalem, a place of resort at particular seasons, *(at one of which the first great increase took place)* where the converts were many of them *from a distance*, and *soon to return* to their respective countries; where *persecution*, and *zeal* to propagate the gospel, combined to *disperse them abroad.*" In Acts xxi. 20, the phrase " many myriads," is evidently an indefinite one. Nothing but the spirit of controversy could impel any sensible reader to maintain that it is generally used definitely in the New Testament.

" Thou seest, brother," said the elders, "how many thousands of Jews there are that believe; and they are all zealous of the law." There is, moreover, no necessity to limit this language to those permanently residing at Jerusalem. Does it not, with more propriety, refer to the believing portion of the *Jewish nation* generally, great numbers of whom were now come up to the feast of Pentecost; for we find Paul hurrying, that if possible, he might be in time for it. See Acts xx. 16, and xxi.

15, 16. See an Admirable Lecture on part of Acts xv. by the Rev. Greville Ewing, published 30 years ago.

But is it not expressly said, that this multitude, these very myriads, "must needs *come together?*" Oh, but, replies Dr. M'Leod, the multitude means nothing more than the deputies from the several churches, or in other words, the Presbytery of Jerusalem! Well, what reader of the Bible would have thought *that*, if some lynx-eyed Presbyterian had not discovered it! Alas, alas, the spirit of Neology is not confined to the Infidels of Germany! It is truly lamentable to see an Orthodox Presbyterian labouring with most perverse ingenuity to evade the force of the plainest statements in the Word of God. Who would think of calling a meeting of the Presbytery of Belfast, "the multitude coming together?" Was even the meeting of the Synod of Ulster ever so designated? The Scripture says, "the Apostles and elders, with the whole church," &c. The phrase, "with the whole church," says Dr. M'Leod, is an *expletive*, a redundant expression, a mere pleonasm, and means nothing more than the Apostles and elders. This is criticism with a vengeance! Let the impartial reader compare the angry special pleading and text-torturing ingenuity of Dr. M'Leod with the calm and judicious observations of Mr. Ewing on this passage, and we have no fears as to the conclusion at which he will arrive.

Thus have we not the shadow of authority for ecclesiastical courts in the Bible. Neither can they derive any support from the history of the primitive church. The testimony of MOSHEIM is most unqualified and decisive as to the independency of all the churches of the first century. See his History, vol. i., cent. 1, p. 2., chap. 2, sect. 14.

But this learned and impartial writer enters more fully into this interesting subject in his valuable work ("De Rebus Christianorum ante Constantum Magnum") "On the affairs of the Christians before Constantine the Great." One of the sections of this book is thus headed—"Omnes ecclesiæ primæ ætatis independentes"—"All the churches of the first century INDEPENDENT." This position he supports at great length, and establishes in the most convincing manner. He enters, in the course of the discussion, into a critical examination of Acts xv. in connexion with other passages; and with resistless force, rends away from pope, prelate, and presbyter, every shred of argument by which they could hang their councils, convocations, and synods, on the assembly of the church at Jerusalem. He maintains, that in this century the churches never met, by their bishops and deputies, to hold provincial councils or synods, for the purpose of enacting laws for the whole body, or deciding the controversies that might have arisen; but that, on the contrary, the churches were strictly *independent*—governing "*themselves without any foreign assistance, or external authority*"—"*seque ipsae sine alieno auxilio et externa quadam auctoritate* gubernabant."

Thus the cause of Independency is triumphant—"our enemies themselves being judges." While we have the MOSHEIMS and the CAMPBELLS of other denominations to fight our battles, we need not fear the puny efforts of anonymous assailants. The force of truth has wrung even from the prejudice of MILNER an admission in our favour. "Usher's plan of reduced episcopacy," says he, in his History of the Church, cent. 2d, chap. i., "seems to come the nearest to the plan of the primitive churches. At first, indeed, or for some time, church governors were *only of two ranks,* presbyters and deacons, and the term *bishop* was confounded with that of *presbyter.*" But even when something like episcopacy began to make its appearance, when the presiding pastor began to assume, and had gradually conceded to him, a controlling influence over the six, or eight, or perhaps twelve ministers, that itinerated around him—there was still but *one church.* "One bishop, one altar," was a proverbial saying among the early christians. To erect the second *communion table* within the jurisdiction of a bishop, was considered nothing less than the abominable sin of schism. The bishop dispensed the ordinances, and knew personally all the members of his flock, without whose consent, obtained in their church meeting, he neither exercised discipline, nor transacted any other important business relating to the community over which he presided. The reader who wishes for full and satisfactory information on this most important question, should study Lord Chancellor King's "Inquiry into the Constitution, &c., of the Primitive Church." To Mr. Carlile's arguments, founded on Matt. xviii. 17, his opponents have not even attempted an answer. It only remains that I should offer a few remarks on .

CHURCH COMMUNION.

Some persons deem it a matter of regret, that Mr. Carlile should have given rise to this controversy by the publication of his discourse. I cannot agree with them. There never was any reformation in the church, which was not accompanied by some incidental evils. The faithful antagonist of error must expect to be represented and treated as a "troubler of Israel," and a "sower of dissension." It was the cry raised by Jews against the Apostles; by Papists against the Reformers, and by Episcopalians against the Puritans. Why should we not examine the scriptures for ourselves? Why should we not speak and publish our sentiments freely? Is it possible that fair and open discussion is to be stifled in Belfast? The spirit of enquiry, however, *will not* be put down! Like a giant refreshed with wine, it is rising in its might, and where is the man who dares resist its march? The strongholds of corruption are tottering—the guards are trembling for their livings, while the birds of darkness are ominously shrieking, as they fly before the light. Society is about to be exorcised— the satanic legion must be expelled, and we shall speedily see the professing church, "sitting at the feet of Jesus, clothed, and in her right mind." For, alas, she has been drunk and delirious with the cup of abomination, which the State gave her to drink in the day of their fatal espousals! Let not, therefore, the whispers of carnal prudence deter the friends of truth and righteousness from lifting up their voice like a trumpet, until the Sword of the Spirit has completely dissevered the adulterous connexion. "There is a tide in the affairs of men." Let us now take it at its ebb, and we shall soon see *High Church* a naked hulk, deserted, and stranded behind us, while the voluntary churches float onward at the command of their divine Commodore, conquering, and to conquer the world.

I assert that Mr. Carlile has rendered important service to the cause of Christ in this controversy. He has compelled his opponents, virtually, to relinquish one of the most pernicious principles that ever Satan employed to corrupt the church of Christ; namely, that an *Orthodox profession* and *external morality*—(even these, it would seem, are not always insisted on,)—and not satisfactory evidence of *regeneration*, should be regarded as the terms of communion. This is the damning principle of all state churches. This is the principle that confounds the church and the world—that pollutes the sanctuary of the Lord —that sanctifies a heartless and selfish morality—that confirms the soul-destroying delusion of the self-righteous—that fixes the seal of ecclesiastical approbation on the inoperative faith of the Sandemanian—that invites into the fold, the thief, the robber, and the wolf—that confounds faith and infidelity, and impiously endeavours to yoke together CHRIST and Balial. It is mournful to reflect, how this fatal principle has been cherished by Presbyterian Churches; and even still they cling to it, after all the bitter fruits it has produced! It has desolated their once pure and prosperous churches in England; it has withered the vine planted in Geneva, which flourished like the cedars of Lebanon, and sent out its glory unto all lands; it settled like a plague spot on the Presbyterian Church in this country, until there was scarcely any life remaining. Oh, that they would reject this deadly principle—that imitating the glorious example of their brethren in America, they would unite with the Congregational body, in *witnessing, as churches*, against an unbelieving world; in building up the battlements of Zion, so that the foes of our KING should not sit down at his table, and riot in his palaces.

Why are regeneration, faith, love, pardon, justification, the renewal of the heart, the fruits of the spirit, and other scriptural expressions, discarded as tests of discipleship, to make room for the ambiguous and equivocal phrase, "a sound sound profession and a blameless life?" Why is it that " notorious *immorality*," and " gross transgressions"— ("*mortal sins*, I suppose; if Romanists were better acquainted with certain Protestant churches, they might apply the *argumentum ad hominem* with much greater effect)—why is it that those more flagrant and scandalous outbreakings of corruption, should be exhibited as the only things on account of which a man should be *authoritatively* shut out from the privileges of the church? Why are no ecclesiastical anathemas, no synodical fulminations, made to light on the path of the dry moralist, the sleek hypocrite, and the *prudent* sinner? In the language of an excellent minister of Christ,* on this subject I would say, " Verily, there must be *guilt somewhere!*"

But we are told that Independents presume to search the heart; and this presumption is blasphemous. Certainly: but what Independent has defended such presumption? Do we not again and again, most solemnly disclaim any such pretentions? But if we disclaim the divine prerogative of searching the heart, is there no other way of ascertaining the state of the soul before God? May we not know the nature of a tree by its *fruits*, though we cannot see and examine the root? And

---

* The Rev. J. Morgan.

does not scripture say, "Ye shall *know them* by their fruits?" A fountain may be hid from our view, but we can ascertain its quality by examining the streams which issue from it. "Doth a fountain send forth at the same place sweet water and bitter?" Is it not written, "By this shall ALL MEN *know* that ye are my disciples, if ye have love one to another?" Why do the people of God love one another? Because they recognize one another as brethren in Christ. Why does the world hate believers? Because they take knowledge of them that they have been with Christ. In fine, does not the Bible, especially the Epistles, every where *assume the fact*, that the people of God *do* know one another?

It is really very uncandid to blame Congregationalists for doing that, as churches, which their pious opponents are continually doing, as individuals. Do they not speak of some of their acquaintances as converted, and of others as unconverted, and regulate their social intercourse accordingly? Do they not, in choosing husbands or wives, look for the evidences of regeneration? "This fundamental principle of our system," says Mr. Carlile, in his Letter, "has been fully recognized in one important application of it by your Synod in the recent appointment of its 'Theological Examination Committee;' that committee professes to inquire into the *personal piety* of candidates for the ministry. Now God alone can 'judge the heart of a student, and yet you inquire into his personal piety.'" Here then is our principle acted upon by the Synod; why not extend its application to the members of the church?

I have already alluded to an admirable sermon, published by the Rev. James Morgan. I was struck with the following beautiful passage:—"Bring together four converts to Christ from the utmost extremities of north, east, south, and west. Let their manners, education, and habits, be the most dissimilar and contrary. Suppose them different in every thing but one, the love of Christ. Yet place them at one table, and give them a common language, and they will *understand* one another, *love* one another, enter into all the *fellowship of brethren*, rejoice in the same joys, and sympathize in the same sorrows."

What! is this possible? Strangers from the four extremities of the world, in all earthly things dissimilar, *know* one another to be *christians*, and *love* one another as *brethren!* Yes, blessed be God, it is even so. But had I the honour of Mr. Morgan's acquaintance, I might ask him, if all this be true, what is to hinder people of the same country, of the same town, of the same parish, or congregation, to *know* one another to be believers, and *love* one another as *brethren?* If the force of christian sympathy overcomes at once all the repellent peculiarities arising from climate, habit, education, &c., so that the heart inspired by divine love breaks through every impediment, in order to unite itself to that of a brother, why, in the name of common sense, should it not do so, when there is nothing to check the outflowing of its affection, but every thing conspires to draw it forth? In the same discourse, Mr. Morgan writes, "Let them not attempt to judge the heart; nor make their knowledge of regeneration a term of communion." What a pity that attachment to a system should lead so amiable, sensible, and pious a writer, into such inconsistencies and contradictions! Can there possibly *be* communion between the members of a church, unless they are satisfied in their minds that those among whom they intimately associate as christians, are *really* christians—that is, that they are *regenerated?* Is not this senseless logomachy—this strife about words, unworthy of christians? Away with it, then, and let our minds rest upon *things*.

Why, according to Mr. Morgan, it is not a cold, prying, criticising, anatomising process of "judging the heart" at all; but the powerful attraction of an uncontrollable smypathy, which binds soul to soul, almost instantaneously; a kind of instinctive knowledge of a stranger's inmost feelings; a suddenly awakened consciousness of kindred; the exercise of an affection, which, spurning ceremony, springs to the embrace of its object, and clings there with a force stronger than death. It is true that consummate hypocrites—wolves in sheeps' clothing, may sometimes escape our utmost vigilance, but our hands are clear from their blood.

It is with great reluctance I quote another passage from Mr. Morgan's Sermon; but truth demands it. It is important, as showing the embarrassments, the difficulties, and distress, that beset the most godly and influential minister, in congregations where our principles, in regard to church communion, are practically rejected.

"The preacher," he observes, "can speak feelingly on this theme, having more than once been placed in circumstances of the utmost perplexity and distress. He has been called to minister to societies, among whom christian discipline *was almost unknown*. To have introduced it immediately and vigorously, would *more than have endangered their existence*. He felt, that, to a great extent, there was no choice left, but either *to abandon it,* or renounce his charge. And it is only *after years (!)* of anxious solicitude, and careful preparation, that he now—(this was spoken in June, 1832,)—*begins to hope (!!)* that an *an attempt may (!!!)* be made to bring his people under the influence of christian discipline."

I will not venture to analyse this passage, or to educe from it those inferences which it seems to suggest. It might hurt Mr. Morgan's feelings; and I would not give him the slightest pain, if I could possibly avoid it, and yet be faithful to the truth. We may learn from it, however, the necessity of caution in commencing *personal* hostilities against others. We should look at home, before we begin to cast stones at our neighbours. If Mr. Carlile had no more christian forbearance than his assailants, he might retort with fearful effect; he might place Mr. Morgan in a most painful dilemma! But I trust he has not so learned Christ as to render evil for evil. I do most cordially sympathise with Mr. Morgan. Alas, for those holy men of God, that are struggling and groaning in the chains of an unscriptural system! "If they do these things *in a green tree,* what shall be done in the dry?"

To pious Presbyterians, I would say, in conclusion—Dear brethren, lay these things to heart, and let them furnish matter for your petitions at the throne of grace. We have no wish to sow dissensions in your congregations, nor to proselyte your people; but we earnestly desire to see the professing church brought back to its primitive purity and simplicity. Remember, I beseech, you the words of the Apostle—"Be not unequally yoked together with unbelievers; for what fellowship hath righteousness with unrighteousness? and what communion hath light with darkness? and what concord hath Christ with Belial? or what part hath he that believeth with an infidel? and what agreement hath the temple of God with idols? Wherefore, come out from among them, and be ye separate, saith the Lord, and touch not the unclean thing; and I will receive you, and will be a father unto you, and ye shall be my sons and daughters, saith the Lord Almighty." To our opponents in the *Orthodox Presbyterian,* I would give a parting word of advice, from the Song of Hannah—"Talk no more, *so exceeding proudly;* let not arrogancy come out of your mouth; for the LORD is a God of knowledge, and by HIM actions are weighed."

FINIS.

MORMONISM OR THE BIBLE?

A QUESTION FOR THE TIMES.

BY A CAMBRIDGE CLERGYMAN.

CAMBRIDGE:
PUBLISHED BY
T. DIXON, MARKET STREET;
SOLD BY
WERTHEIM & MACINTOSH, 24, PATERNOSTER ROW.

MDCCCLII.

MORMONISM OR THE BIBLE?

A QUESTION FOR THE TIMES.

When any religious doctrine or system is proposed to us, our duty is to compare it with God's written Word, and to accept or reject it according as it agrees with or differs from the Bible. Our Blessed Lord himself, though he came to introduce a new dispensation, though he spake as never man spake, and wrought almost countless miracles, yet acknowledged and appealed to the Scriptures of the former dispensation.* And his Apostles followed the same course. The Jews of Beræa are commended because they "searched the Scriptures" of the Old Testament "daily, whether those things" which Paul and Silas taught them "were so."†

Now there has sprung up in America during the present century a sect commonly called "Mormonites," but who call themselves "the Church of Jesus Christ of Latter-day Saints." Some of these persons have come over to England, and are diligently spreading abroad in our towns and villages strange claims and new doctrines, which they require us, at the peril of our souls, to receive. Let us then take with regard to them the course pointed out above. Let us see whether it can be Mormonism *and* the Bible; and if not, which

* Luke xxiv. 25—27, 32, 44—48; John v. 39, 46.
† Acts xvii. 11. See also Acts i. 16; ii. 16, 25; &c.

it ought to be, Mormonism, *or* the Bible? The Mormonites themselves appeal to the Bible, though they greatly err in denying that it is the *only* and *sufficient* standard of religious truth. They profess, however, to prove their system by Scripture; and on this ground we meet them. "To the law and to the testimony: if they speak not according to this word, it is because there is no light in them."*

We shall shew that Mormonism is opposed to the Bible in these four particulars:—

    I. Its Pretensions;
    II. Its Origin;
    III. Its Authority;
    IV. Its Doctrines.

I. *Its Pretensions.*

1. It pretends to be the only Church of Christ upon earth. Nay, more than this, to be the only one that has been upon earth since the second century! Hear the words of one of its so-called apostles:—

"Let the reader not be startled when I tell him that something like fifteen thousand millions of the human race have gone down to their graves without complying with these rules" [of adoption into the kingdon of God]. "Do not be angry or prejudiced when I candidly inform you, that neither man or woman on the great eastern hemisphere, during the long period of more than seventeen hundred years, has been legally adopted into the kingdom of God. No person among them from the second to the nineteenth century of the Christian era obeyed the gospel, or was born into the kingdom. All were aliens and strangers, and such a thing as the kingdom of God was not known among them."†

Again:—

"No churches, either among the Papists or Protestants, have taught all the first principles of the gospel in their proper order. By this we know they are not the church of God. God is not with them. Their sins are not forgiven them. The Holy Ghost is not given to them.................The apostate churches now on the earth have neither inspired apostles no

---

* Is. viii. 20.

†"The Kingdom of God," by Orson Pratt, one of the twelve apostles of the Church of Jesus Christ of Latter-day Saints. Part ii., p. 2.

prophets, nor any other inspired officers among them, neither do they consider them necessary; and yet without inspiration or revelation—without immersion for remission of sins, or the ordinance for the gift of the Spirit, they have the bold impudence to call themselves Christian churches. But they have nothing to do with Christ, neither has Christ anything to do with them, only to pour out upon them the plagues written. He has not spoken to any of them for many centuries, neither will he speak to them, only in his wrath, and in the fierceness of his anger, when he riseth up to overthrow, to root up, and to destroy them utterly from the earth."*

And must we then indeed believe that not one man of all the millions that have lived in our world during the last 1700 years has been saved? That all the saints and martyrs, and confessors, of whom we have heard and read; all the holy, happy Christians whom we ourselves have known and loved, have perished everlastingly? The writer seems himself almost to shrink from such a conclusion, for he says elsewhere:—

"Neither can they enjoy the promised salvation in all its fulness, but must be rewarded according to their works and the opportunities they have enjoyed, in some of the mansions or kingdoms inferior in glory to the kingdom possessed by the ancient saints, who obeyed the law and enjoyed the promised blessings."†

But not to urge that such an idea is a pure invention of the writer's, not only unsanctioned by, but opposed to, Holy Scripture, we say, if words mean anything, then if "*their sins are not forgiven them,*" if "*the Holy Ghost is not given to them,*" if Christ has not "*anything to do with them, only to pour out upon them the plagues written,*" they must be *lost*. Many other passages in a strain not of tender pity and Christian love for the erring and the perishing, but of vulgar abuse and bitter invective against all who are without the pale of Mormonism, might be quoted. But these will suffice to shew that the Mormonites pretend to be the only true church that is or has been since the second century.

* Ib. p. 8.   † Ib. part iv., p. 8.

But now what saith the Scripture?

(i.) It teaches us that God has always had *a faithful remnant—a church upon earth.*

He had so when the whole earth was corrupt, in the days of Noah, Gen. vi.

He had so when the Jewish nation was corrupt—
> In the days of Elijah, 1 Kings, xix. 18;
> ——————Malachi, c. iii. 16;
> ——————St. Paul, Rom. xi. 5.

(ii.) Our Saviour Christ distinctly promises that his church shall continue *to the end of the world.*

In Matt. xvi. 18, he says of it, "the gates of hell shall not prevail against it." And yet we are to be told that Satan has prevailed to sweep the church from the face of the earth for 1700 out of the 1800 years that have elapsed since those words were spoken! Again, we have his well-known promise: "Lo, I am with you alway, even unto the end of the world."* We cannot possibly confine these words to the Apostles, because they did not live to the end of the world. They were spoken to them *as the representatives of the church.* If, then, Christ was to be with the church alway unto the end of the world, there must *be a church alway unto the end of the world,* and a church *upon earth;* for the idea that Christ here promised to be with his disciples "after the period of the death of their mortal bodies,"† is not conveyed by the words; (it would have been "ye shall be with me," not "I am with you:" it would have been "for ever and ever," not only "to the end of the world;") and is moreover clean contrary to the context, which connects the promise with the great command which is binding on the church in all ages,—"Go ye into all the world, and preach the gospel to every creature."

We have shewn, then, that the Mormonite pretensions to be the only church are opposed to Scripture,

---

* Matt. xxviii. 20.
† Divine Authenticity of the Book of Mormon, No. iii., pp. 43, 44.

and we do not scruple to add, impious and blasphemous. It is a fearful thing to "make God a liar," and to curse those "whom God hath not cursed."

2. The *pretensions* of Mormonism go to subvert all existing civil government.

"One of the twelve apostles" thus writes:—

"For 1700 years the nations upon the eastern hemisphere have been entirely destitute of the "*Kingdom of God*,"—entirely destitute of a true and legal government,—entirely destitute of officers legally authorized to rule and govern. All the emperors, kings, princes, presidents, lords, nobles, and rulers, during that long night of darkness, have acted without authority, not one of them was called or anointed a king, or prince, by the God of heaven,—not one of them received his office or appointment by him,—not one of them has received revelations or laws from him,—not one of them has received any communication whatsoever from the rightful Sovereign— the great King. Their authority is all assumed, it originated in man."*

Now when we turn to Rom. xiii., we find another *Apostle* writing thus of *heathen* rulers:—

"Let every soul be subject unto the higher powers. *For there is no power but of God: the powers that be are ordained of God.* Whosoever therefore resisteth the power, resisteth *the ordinance of God.*"†

Now, supposing, for argument's sake, that we Christians are as bad as the Mormonites make us out to be—as bad as *heathen*, just mark the contrast. The Apostle of Christ says of *heathen* powers, they "*are ordained of God.*" The apostle of Mormonism says of *heathen* powers (if you will), "Their authority is all assumed, *it originated in man.*" Whom shall we believe, St. Paul or Mr. Orson Pratt? God, or man? "Yea, let God be true, but every man a liar." How dare we follow men, who thus flatly contradict the word of God?

The *pretensions* of Mormonism then, both as regards the church and the state, are opposed to the Bible.

* Kingdom of God, part i., p. 1. †See Rom. xiii. 1—6.

II. The same is true of its *Origin*.

The founder of Mormonism was Joseph Smith, the so-called Mormon *prophet*. Now we have this caution given us by Christ himself: "*Beware of false prophets.*" But how are we to know whether a prophet be true or false? It is added: "*Ye shall know them BY THEIR FRUITS.*"* Let us then apply this test to Joseph Smith, the Mormon prophet. We shall not give a connected history of him, but merely state some plain facts.

1. And first, what was his early history? The following account is given of the family on the very best authority :†—

"For breach of contracts, for non-payment of debts and borrowed money, and for duplicity with their neighbours, the family was notorious; and their whole object seems to have been to live without work, upon the industry of others. In this school of villainy our prophet was trained from a child, *and finally became the most distinguished of his vagrant family for cunning and unscrupulous audacity.*"‡

When about 17 years old (in 1822) he got possession of a curious stone, which had been found in digging a well, and pretended to be able to discover by its help where gold was hid. In this way he duped and cheated many persons. "For the space of four years he led a wandering life, without any ostensible business, and *was once or twice arrested as a common vagabond.*"§ About this time he contrived to get recommended to a Miss Hale, the daughter of a respectable man, *with whom he eloped during her father's absence.* I read in the Bible, "If any provide not for his own, and specially for those of his own house, he hath denied the faith, and is worse than an infidel."‖ And, again,

---

* See also the whole passage. Matt. vii. 15—20.
† We quote from a valuable work, entitled "The Prophet of the Nineteenth Century," by the Rev. Henry Caswall, M.A., Professor of Divinity in Kemper College, Missouri. Mr. Caswall, besides the advantage of personal observation, has consulted the principal works both for and against Mormonism.
‡ Caswall, p. 29.   § Ib. p. 30.   ‖ 1 Tim. v. 8.

"We beseech you, brethren........that ye study to be quiet, and to do your own business, and to work with your own hands, as we commanded you."*

2. We will now give a few facts connected with the pretended discovery and publication of the "Book of Mormon," or "Golden Bible." The substance of what follows is stated on oath by one Peter Ingersol, a companion of Smith:—

In the course of the Autumn (1827), while walking in the woods, he happened to find some beautifully white sand, washed up by a stream. He tied some of it up in his frock and took it home; and when his family asked what he had there, he gravely said that it was the 'Golden Bible.' To his surprise they believed him, and begged to see the book. He answered that no one could see it with the naked eye and live; but that if they liked to take the consequences, he would shew it them. They declined and ran from the room in great terror. 'Now,' said the prophet with an oath, 'I have got the fools fixed, and I will carry out the fun.'† He then invented a story, which was altered and enlarged from time to time, to the effect that he had seen visions of an angel, who directed him to go to a certain place, where he would find, buried in a stone box in the earth, the Golden Bible. He discovered, and was afterwards permitted to take away with him the book, which was 'engraved on plates which had the appearance of gold.' These plates 'were filled on both sides with engravings in Egyptian characters, and bound together in a volume, as the leaves of a book.' This book he pretended to translate, sitting behind a thick curtain, while one Martin Harris (whom he had persuaded to believe his story, and to provide money for his maintenance and the publication of the work) wrote down the words from his mouth. To the book as published is prefixed the testimony of eleven witnesses, who assert that they saw the plates, and some of them that they 'handled' them.‡ Three saw them first, and afterwards the other eight, though '*Smith had originally revealed that three persons only were to be permitted to behold the plates.*'

But, we observe, that these witnesses were persons of the most worthless character, and all of them *in-*

---

* 1 Thess. iv. 11. See also 2 Thess. iii. 10—12.
† Oath of Peter Ingersol. See Caswall, pp. 35, 6.
‡ See "The Book of Mormon." Liverpool: published by Orson Pratt, 15, Wilton Street.

terested in the success of the imposture. We have no *respectable, independent, disinterested* witness. Again, they state that the engravings on the plates were shewn them " by the power of God, and not of man ;" and " that an angel of God came down from heaven"* to shew them. And one of the witnesses, when questioned, said, that he " saw them with the eye of faith, though at the time they were covered over with a cloth."! Now where, we ask, was the need of " the power of God," or " the coming of an angel," or " the eye of faith," to see these plates, if they really existed? Why could they not be seen, as other things are? Why have we not the testimony of some straightforward, honest, disinterested men? The answer is clear—because the whole thing is an impudent and wicked imposture. How unspeakably awful it is thus daringly to insult God, and trifle with holy things;—to set forth as a revelation from heaven, such a gross and intentional fabrication!

But one fact more. The Book of Mormon is based upon a historical romance or tale, written by a Mr. Solomon Spaulding. That romance was written in 1812, and is " similar in all its leading features to the historical portions of the Book of Mormon." That the manuscript of it " came into the hands of the founder of Mormonism, and that it was made subservient to the purposes of a vile imposition, is as certain as that the book of Mormon exists."† These facts speak for themselves: and yet the book which had so worthy an origin, we are to reverence no less than the Inspired Word of God! Joseph Smith is to be received as a prophet equal in authority to the Divine Saviour himself!

3. It is not our purpose to pursue the history of Smith. One or two facts will shew that he did not afterwards improve.

In 1835 he and others formed a mercantile house,

---

* Ib. † Caswall, p. 25.

and bought goods to the amount of some £22,000. When pay-day came, they were unable to meet their liabilities. They therefore set up a *bank, without a Charter*, (which was refused them by the government,) and issued notes in large quantities. The holders of these notes getting alarmed, came to the bank to know what was its capital; but Smith was ready for them. He had filled one box with dollars, and about two hundred similar boxes with heavy rubbish. The one containing the silver he opened, and by allowing persons to feel the weight of the others, led them to suppose that they too were full of silver. Thus the holy prophet escaped for a time; but in a few months the bank broke, and Smith "having swindled the community to a prodigious extent," took to flight, closely, though fruitlessly, pursued by the officers of justice.

" Smith had publicly prophesied in 1841 in the presence of thousands, that his old enemy Boggs, the ex-governor of Missouri, would die by *violent hands* within a year. He now offered a reward of 500 dollars to several of the Danites,* if they would assassinate the gentleman in question. One of the terrible band accordingly proceeded more than 200 miles to Independence, where the ex-governor resided. Smith being asked by Bennett, the Mayor, to inform him whither this Danite had gone, promptly replied, with a significant nod, that "he was gone to fulfil prophecy." In the course of two months, the Danite returned to Nauvoo; and on the day following his arrival the news reached that place that the ex-governor had been assassinated. The Danite who had previously been miserably poor, now appeared in possession of an elegant carriage and horses, and with his pockets filled with gold."†

"Smith had already taught the doctrine, that "the blessings of Jacob were granted to him ;" in consequence

* The Danites were a particular band of Mormons, whose character and employment may be guessed from what follows.
† Caswall, pp. 225, 6.

of which he asserted that he might indulge, like David and Solomon, in unrestricted polygamy. In conformity with these instructions of their *infallible* head, many English and American women, whose husbands or fathers had been sent by the prophet on distant missions, were induced to become his "'spiritual wives,' 'believing it to be the will of God.'"*

And now we return to our Lord's rule—" By their *fruits* ye shall know him." The *fruits* of J. Smith were *idleness, lying, blasphemy, cheating, murder*, and *adultery*. Was he then a true or a false prophet? Oh beware,—as you value your souls,—beware of *false prophets!*

Thus opposed not only to the Bible, but to reason and morality, is Mormonism in its author and its origin.

III. We are next to shew that it is opposed to Holy Scripture in respect of *its Authority*. Its advocates declare that their authority is *divine:* and in proof of this, they

    1. Pretend to work *miracles;*
    2. Assert that they have the gift of *prophecy;*
    3. Lay claim to *revelation;*
    4. Appeal to *Scripture.*

1. Of the alleged miracles of Mormonism we do not believe a single one. There is no sufficient evidence for them. They are things done in a corner, amongst their own people; and testified for the most part by members of their own sect. Indeed it has been truly said of a number of the Mormon miracles of healing, that " any one who has seen a list of the cures advertised in recommendation of certain quack medicines, has seen the counterpart of it." Why do not these men work miracles, as our Lord and his Apostles did, in the face of day and in the sight of the people?—" a notable miracle," manifest to all the people: which the rulers " cannot deny."† Why not go into some of our large public hospitals and there perform their

---

* Ib. p. 226. See Note A.   † See Acts iii. and iv.

cures? So again, if they have the gift of tongues indeed, how comes it to pass that they confine their preaching to places where *English* is spoken? Ought not foreign nations, and the perishing heathen to " hear them speak *in their tongues* the wonderful works of God? But even if they could work miracles it would not of itself be sufficient. The Bible plainly speaks of miracles which are not from God.* A Mormon apostle writes : " There are two kinds of miracles ; first, those wrought by the power of God ; and second, those wrought by the power of the devil. Wherever miracles are wrought by the power of God, *there* will be found a true and righteous doctrine, unmixed with error: wherever miracles are wrought by the power of the devil, *there* will be found more or less false doctrine."† We have seen, and shall further see, the doctrine and whole system of Mormonism to be false, unrighteous, and full of error. If, then, it has miracles, by whose power must they be wrought? There is one most solemn passage which we recommend to the serious and prayerful consideration of all who are being deluded by the lying wonders of Mormonism, because it shews how fearfully men may be deceived in this respect : " And then shall that Wicked be revealed, whom the Lord shall consume with the spirit of his mouth, and shall destroy with the brightness of his coming: Even him, whose coming is after the working of Satan, with all power and signs, and lying wonders, and with all deceivableness of unrighteousness in them that perish because they received not the love of the truth, that they might be saved. And for this cause God shall send them strong delusion, that they should believe a lie : that they all might be damned who believed not the truth, but had pleasure in unrighteousness."‡

2. With regard to the *prophecies* of Mormonism,

* See Matt. xxiv. 24 ; Rev. xiii. 13, 14.
† Divine Authenticity of the Book of Mormon, by Orson Pratt, No. v., pp. 1—3.
‡ 2 Thess. ii. 8—12.

we believe them as little as we do its miracles; and for the same reasons,—viz., that they are obscure and have no sufficient evidence. But, were they true, they would only remind us of a passage in the book of Deuteronomy, which reads thus: "If there arise among you a prophet, or a dreamer of dreams, and giveth thee a sign or a wonder, and the sign or the wonder come to pass, whereof he spake unto thee, saying, Let us go after other gods, which thou hast not known, and let us serve them; Thou shalt not hearken unto the words of that prophet, or that dreamer of dreams: for the Lord your God proveth you, to know whether ye love the Lord your God with all your heart and with all your soul."* The Mormon prophets "speak to thrust us out of the way which the Lord our God commanded us to walk in;" therefore, whatever be their gifts, they are not to be listened to.

3. As for their claim to *revelation*, we say, God cannot contradict himself. What he reveals in one way, cannot be clean contrary to what he reveals in another. We know and are sure that the Bible is a revelation from God. But the so-called revelations of Mormonism are, as we have seen, *clean contrary* to the Bible; therefore they cannot be from God. These men talk much of angels appearing to them. We read of a prophet who perished miserably because he disobeyed "*the word of the Lord,*" through listening to another prophet, who said to him, "*an angel spake unto me* by the word of the Lord," but who "*lied* unto him."† Let us beware of disobeying "the word of the Lord,"—his written word, through listening to those who tell us that *angels have spoken to them*, but who *lie unto us*. It is an inspired Apostle who says—and it would be well if the apostles of Mormonism would ponder the words—"Though we, or *an angel from heaven*, preach any other gospel unto you than that which we have preached unto you, let him be accursed."‡

*See Deut. xiii. 1—5; also Matt. vii. 22, 3.   † 1 Kings xiii.
‡ Gal. i. 8.

4. But they *appeal to Scripture*. Into this point we shall enter a little more fully, because it is the chief object of this tract to shew how Mormonism and the Bible are at variance.

So far then from gaining authority from Scripture,

(i.) They *contradict* Scripture. This we have proved abundantly already, and shewn from their own works that Mormonism and the Bible cannot both be true.

(ii.) They *pervert* Scripture. They tell us that "the perfect agreement between the predictions of Isaiah (chap. xxix.) and Mr. Smith's account of the finding and translation of the Book of Mormon, is another collateral proof that he was divinely commissioned."* Now we ask any unprejudiced person to read carefully through the first four verses of Is. xxix., and say whether they do not all refer to *one and the same* city. But in a Mormon publication now before me, I find it asserted, that in those verses "the prophet predicts, first, the distress that should come upon Ariel; and, secondly, predicts another event that should be unto the Lord as Ariel. This last event is expressed in these words, "*And it shall be unto me* AS *Ariel :*"† And then we are told that, according to the Book of Mormon, this latter event related to "the nation of Nephites, who were a remnant of Joseph inhabiting ancient America"! Verily we need a *prophet* to teach us that in the short verse, "Yet I will distress Ariel, and there shall be heaviness and sorrow: and it shall be unto me as Ariel," the first part refers to Jerusalem, and the last to the nation of Nephites, who were a remnant of Joseph inhabiting ancient America! Is it not clear that Isaiah, having called Jerusalem by the unusual name "Ariel," explains the reason of his giving it that name by the words "it shall be unto me *as* Ariel?" In the same way he calls Jerusalem "Sodom" and "Gomorrah," because it was *as* Sodom and *as* Gomorrah in wickedness, as well as almost "*as* Sodom"

* Divine Authority, by Orson Pratt, p. 8. † Reply to "Remarks on Mormonism," p. 11.

and "*like unto* Gomorrah" in punishment.* But as the author, commenting on a place in Ezekiel, tells us what he "conceives to be the true rendering of the passage," it is a pity that he did not here also refer to his *Hebrew* Bible. He would have found that the word translated "it shall be" is a *feminine* verb, and can only have for its nominative case the feminine noun "city" in v. 1; so that it really is—" The city where David dwelt shall be to me as Ariel."

But we are further told that the 3rd and 4th verses of the chapter refer to the same "remnant of Joseph;" that "the words of their ancient prophets speak out of the ground," and "whisper out of the dust" to the ears of the present generation, revealing, in a very "familiar" (!) manner, the history of ancient America, which before was entirely unknown to the nations."†

Again :—

"But the words of the prophets among the remnant of Joseph have spoken from the ground, and their written '*speech*' has whispered out of the dust. Isaiah declares, that it shall be '*as the voice of one that hath a familiar spirit.*' It was not to be the voice of a distant, vague, uncertain spirit, but 'as a *familiar spirit*,' one that can be familiarly understood, and that, too, by the most ordinary capacity."‡

A more gross and impious perversion of Scripture than this can hardly be imagined. Not to insist, that, if Jerusalem cannot be at once "Ariel," and "*as* Ariel," then neither can the prophets in question *have* the familiar spirit, and be "*as* one that hath it,"—we say that it is an insult to common sense to tell us that when it is said, "*thy voice shall be as of one that hath a familiar spirit*," it is meant, *thou shalt speak in familiar language*. What reader of his Bible, however ignorant, will believe it for a moment? Is it not perfectly clear that the passage means, that as those who consulted, or pretended to consult, evil spirits or the souls of the dead, used to speak low and mutter, (see Is. viii. 19,) so the Jews, when "brought down,"

* Is. i. 9, 10.   † Divine Auth., p. 9.   ‡ Reply, pp. 11, 12.

should speak as persons in such circumstances are wont to do—in an humble and submissive manner? To refer the passage to the finding of the Book of Mormon at all is a wicked perversion. The writer of the tract says, "the term familiar does not necessarily imply evil." Of course it does not. But the term "familiar spirit" is *always* used in a *bad sense,* and spoken of with *condemnation* in Scripture.*

One more instance we give from the same chapter, in which Mr. Orson Pratt is condemned out of his own mouth. The 11th verse reads thus: "And the vision of all is become unto you as the words of a book that is sealed, which men deliver to one that is learned, saying, Read this, I pray thee: and he saith, I cannot, for it is sealed." (By the way, here is another unfortunate *as.*) On this verse we are informed that if "he (Smith) had sent the book to Professor Anthon, instead of some of the transcribed words it would not have been a fulfilment of the terms of the prophecy; for Isaiah expressly says the "words," and not the book, were to be delivered to the learned."†

Now, is it not plainly absurd to put such a construction upon the passage? Because the word "which" may be plural as well as singular; therefore, in spite of the obvious meaning, in spite of its being said, "Read this," not "these," and answered, "I cannot, for *it is,*" not "they are," "sealed," we are to be told that they are the *words,* not the *book,* that are delivered! But Mr. Pratt has again forgotten to consult the original. He would have found that to be literally, "which they give IT;" which word "*it*" cannot possibly refer to anything but the *book.* Therefore, we must conclude that, to use his own language, "it is not a fulfilment of the terms of the prophecy." Oh that Mormon teachers would weigh well the awful guilt they incur by thus "handling the word of God deceitfully;" and Mormon disciples reflect what must

* See, for instance, Levit. xx. 27; Deut. xviii. 10—12. See Note B. † Reply, p. 12.

be the consequence of following such an antiscriptural system!

(iii.) Once more, the advocates of Mormonism *add to Scripture*. Mr. Orson Pratt takes much pains in attempting to prove that it is neither "unscriptural" nor "unreasonable to expect more revelation;" nay, that "more revelation is indispensably necessary,"—"the Bible and tradition being without further revelation an insufficient guide."* Of *tradition* we have nothing to say, except that we utterly reject its authority in matters of faith. But we most confidently assert, that "Holy Scripture containeth *all things* necessary to salvation."† Mr. Pratt says, that the passage 2 Tim. iii. 14—17, cannot be taken to prove this, because the Holy Scriptures which Timothy had known from a child were those of the Old Testament: so that, if the passage proves anything, it proves too much, viz., that the Old Testament is enough, and, therefore, the New Testament superfluous. But, we answer, St. Paul writes thus: "But continue thou in the things which thou hast learned and hast been assured of, knowing of whom thou hast learned them; and that from a child thou hast known the Holy Scriptures, which are able to make thee wise unto salvation through faith which is in Christ Jesus." Here we take "the things thou hast learned and hast been assured of," to be the doctrines of Christianity taught him by St. Paul,‡ whose own son in the faith he was,§ and with which, the guide of his youth, the Scriptures of the Old Testament perfectly ageeed; for they were "able to make him wise unto salvation *through faith which is in Christ Jesus*." But this is not all; the Apostle adds that important declaration, which applies to the whole of the Bible, and to no other book whatsoever: "All Scripture is given by inspiration of God." To say that this cannot refer to those books of the New

---

* Divine Authenticity of the Book of Mormon.
† 6th Art. of the Ch. of Eng.
‡ c. i. 13; iii. 10.   § 1 Tim. i. 2.

Testament which were written *after* this Epistle, is to deny that St. Paul wrote under the inspiration of the Holy Ghost, who knew that there would be books added, and what they would be; and who therefore declared of all those books, both of the Old and New Testament, which we receive, and "of whose authority was never any doubt in the church," that they are " given by inspiration of God." Of this Scripture St. Paul says, that it is able to make "the man of God perfect, throughly furnished unto all good works." Nay, says Mr. O. Pratt, "It can do no such thing, more revelation is indispensably necessary;" the Bible without it is " an *insufficient* guide." Again, I ask, Whom shall we believe, God or man?

Mr. Pratt denies that the words of St. John (Rev. xxii. 18, 19) can be taken to mean that the canon of Scripture is closed. But considering that the Spirit of God *foresaw* the place which they would occupy in our Bibles, and that they are immediately followed by the declaration, "He which testifieth these things saith, Surely I come quickly," we do think them to be a most solemn warning to all, who at any time before that second coming of Christ, shall dare to add anything to the Scriptures.

Again : our Lord made to his Apostles these two full promises: " But the Comforter, which is the Holy Ghost, whom the Father will send in my name, he shall *teach you all things*, and bring all things to your remembrance, whatsoever I have said unto you."* And, "When he, the Spirit of Truth is come, he will guide you *into* ALL *truth*."† All the truth that the Apostles knew they put on record in their writings, which are of equal authority with their preaching,‡ and that was ALL truth—the whole system of religious truth, as revealed by God in the present dispensation. What more than *all truth* can the new revelation of Mormonism impart? We have our Lord's own word

* John xiv. 26. † Ib. xvi. 13. ‡ See 2 Thess. ii. 2; iii. 14.

for it, that he who believes what the Apostles taught and is baptized "shall be *saved.*"* What more than *salvation* do we want? We are *sure* of salvation in the good old way, in which thousands have been saved and none ever yet perished: "Believe on the Lord Jesus Christ and thou shalt be saved."† Why should we stray into *new* paths of man's inventing, which *may*—not to say *must*—lead us to perdition?

But, even admitting the possibility of new revelation, Mormonism has it not. The New Testament *agrees* with the old; and each successive part of the Bible as it was given *agreed perfectly with all that went before.* It must be so always, for God is the Author of true revelation, and he "is not a man that he should lie, nor the son of man, that he should repent;" with him is "no variableness, neither shadow of turning." How then can Mormonism, which we have repeatedly proved to be flatly opposed to Scripture be, or possess, a new revelation from God? That which contradicts and perverts the Bible, cannot have the same author as the Bible.

There is one more point connected with this adding to Scripture, in which Mr. Orson Pratt is again condemned out of his own mouth. Commenting on Rev. xxii. 18, 19, he says:—

"To add to the words of the book of John's prophecy, means nothing more nor less than to add words or sentences of our own to his book, so as to alter the meaning, and to publish such additions as the words of John. *For Isaiah to have added to the words of the books of Moses, so as to alter their meaning, and to have represented Moses as the author of these altered writings, would have subjected him to a curse.*"‡

We presume that the above statement will hold good, if we write the name of Mr. Orson Pratt for that of Isaiah, thus:—"for Mr. Orson Pratt to have added to the words of Moses, so as to alter their meaning, and to have represented Moses as the author

---

* Mark xvi. 16.   † Acts xvi. 31.
‡ Divine Authenticity, No. i., p. 4.

of these altered writings, would have subjected him to a curse." Now what is the fact? In the second of a course of "Lectures on Faith,"* prefixed to "the Book of Doctrine and Covenants," we find the following:—

"Moses, the historian, has given us the following account of him (man) in the first chapter of the book of Genesis, beginning with the 20th verse, and closing with the 30th. We copy from the new translation. 'And the Lord God said *unto the Only-Begotten who was with him from the beginning,* Let us make man in our image, after our likeness; *and it was done.*........So God created man in his own image, in the image of *the Only-Begotten* created he him.........Again, Genesis ii. 15—20........And the Lord God commanded the man, saying, Of every tree of the garden you may freely eat: but of the tree of knowledge of good and evil, you shall not eat of it, *neither shall you touch it; nevertheless you may choose for yourself, for it is given unto you; but remember that I forbid it,*'" &c.†

By comparing the above passage with the 1st and 2nd chapters of Genesis in the Bible, the reader will see that the parts which we have printed in italics are "*added to the words of the book of Moses, so as to alter their meaning;*" and yet Moses is "*represented as the author of these altered writings,*" for it is said "*Moses, the historian, has given us the following account.*" Surely then, on Mr. Orson Pratt's own shewing, the author of these "Lectures on Faith" is "*subjected to a curse.*"

A little further on in the same lecture we have a wonderful account of the "direct revelation which man received after he was cast out of Eden," copied again from "*the new translation.*" Man is commanded to offer sacrifice, and then an angel tells him—

* It does not clearly appear who is the author of these "Lectures on Faith." If it be J. Smith, his name may be substituted for that of Orson Pratt, in the argument of the text. Be it observed, however, that Mr. Pratt *publishes* and *allows* the book in question.

† The account of Cain and Abel (Gen. iv.) is given in the same way with words and sentences inserted, and yet as quoted from Moses.

"This thing is a similitude of the sacrifice of the Only Begotten of the Father, who is full of grace and truth. And you shall do all that you do in the name of the Son, and you shall repent and call upon God in his name for ever. In that day the Holy Spirit fell upon Adam, and bore record of the Father and the Son."*

Brother Englishmen! will you submit thus to be robbed of that which is the Englishman's birthright,—the Bible—the Word of God? Will you suffer these men to make the Bible speak what they please, by adding to and altering it? Will you be duped by the shallow pretence of a *new translation.* We challenge Mr. Orson Pratt or any other Mormonite to produce a Hebrew copy in which these new words and sentences are to be found. Let them tell us where they come from;—let them *shew* us the *original,* unless, indeed, like the golden plates, it is only to be seen "by the eye of faith." "*Woe unto that man,*" we quote Mr. Pratt's own words, "*who pretends to give a revelation, and is a deceiver, who adds, or diminishes, or alters a revelation which God has given; such cannot escape the threatened judgments of the Almighty.*"†

IV. We are, lastly, to shew that Mormonism is contrary to the Bible in *its Doctrines.* We have only space to take up a few of the many points of *heresy* with which its writings abound.

1. *The nature of God* we will begin with. This awful subject Mormonite writers treat with a flippancy which is perfectly shocking. It is painful and revolting to be compelled to read the remarks upon it contained in "The Kingdom of God." Oh! how unlike the grand and glorious descriptions of God given us in his Word! But let us notice one or two particulars.

(i.) They in effect deny the Godhead of the Father, and of the Son. Mr. Orson Pratt writes:—

"The true God exists both in time and space, and has as much relation to them as man or any other being. He has

* Lectures on Faith, Book of Covenants, p. 12.
† Divine Authenticity, No. i., p. 5.

extension and form, and dimensions, as well as man. He occupies space; has a body, parts, and passions; can go from place to place; can eat, drink, and talk, as well as man. Man resembles him in the features and form of his body, and he does not differ materially in size."*

Now if this be not in *word* and *thought* (if not in deed) to break the Second Commandment, and to incur St. Paul's condemnation of the heathen, who "changed the glory of the uncorruptible God into an image, made like to corruptible man,"† I know not what is. When God asks, "To whom then will ye liken God? or what likeness will ye compare unto him?"‡ is not this to answer, We will liken him to *man*?

But it is added:—

"When he has been seen among men, he has been pronounced, even by the wicked, as one of their own species. *So much did he look like man, that some supposed him to be the carpenter's son.*"

Now we read that when our Lord Jesus Christ was upon earth, some persons said of him, "Is not this the carpenter's son?"§ and this is of course the passage to which Mr. Pratt alludes. We are to understand then, that it was "the true God" (of whom Mr. Pratt is speaking,) *as God only*, who came upon earth, and was supposed to be "the carpenter's son." In other words—God the Father is, and God the Son was *before* he came into the world, exactly what Christ was when on earth. But Christ on earth was not only *like*, but *was man*. "Forasmuch then as the children are partakers of flesh and blood, he also himself likewise took part of the same."‖ Therefore it follows, that not only God the Son, but God the Father, (for we are told that "the two persons were as much alike in form, size, and in every other respect, as fathers and sons of the human race,") *is man;* though our Saviour expressly says, that "God is a Spirit,"¶ and that "a spirit *hath not flesh and bones.*"** To such

* The Kingdom of God, part i., p. 4. † Rom. i. 23.
‡ Is. xl. 18. § Matt. xiii. 55. ‖ Heb. ii. 14. ¶ John iv. 24.
** Luke xxiv. 39.

horrible blasphemy do Mormonite doctrines lead—to say nothing of the absurdity of supposing that our Blessed Lord had a material body "resembling man," before he came into the world, and then in addition took human nature upon him in the womb of the Virgin. But

(ii.) They pervert the doctrine of the Trinity.

In the "Lectures on Faith," it is said:—

"There are *two* personages who constitute the great, matchless, governing, and supreme power, over all things ....they are the Father and the Son............ (the Son) possessing the same mind with the Father, which mind is the Holy Spirit, that bears record of the Father and the Son, and these three are one."

Will any Mormonite give us a text of Scripture to prove that the Holy Spirit is "the mind of the Father and the Son?" But here is a clear denial of the truth that the Holy Ghost is a *Person* distinct from the Father and the Son, which Scripture plainly reveals.* Indeed, the confusion and profanity into which Mormonite writers here fall, is only what we might expect from those who have the daring impiety to follow their own unhallowed fancies and inventions in such high

---

* The Holy Ghost is spoken of as being *grieved*, (Ephes. iv. 30); as *making intercession*, (Rom. viii. 26); as *speaking* to men, (Acts x. 19, 20, and xiii. 2); all of which things shew him to be a Person. See also John xiv. 26; xv. 26, 27; xvi. 7, 8, 13, 14. "All which words are nothing else but so many descriptions of a person; a person hearing, a person receiving, a person testifying, a person speaking, a person reproving, a person instructing." I find, however, that Mr. Orson Pratt will not allow that his doctrine necessarily does away with the *personality* of the Holy Ghost. The following passage needs no comment. "This view of the subject does not necessarily do away a personal spirit, acting in conjunction with the other two persons of the Godhead; for myriads of personal spirits could be organized out of the inexhaustible quantities which exist, and still an abundance would be left to govern and control the various departments of the universe, where these personages could not always be present!"—*Kingdom of God*, part iv., pp. 15, 16. It is to be observed that "Lectures on Faith," as quoted above, say, "there are TWO personages," &c.

and mysterious questions. They deny that the First and Second Persons of the ever-blessed Trinity can be everywhere present; and assert, what we defy them to *prove*, that all the passages that speak of the Omnipresence of God, refer to *the Holy Spirit*. It is said, "God the Father and God the Son cannot be everywhere present; indeed they cannot be even in two places at the same instant." How recklessly these men give God the lie! Our Saviour Christ told the woman of Samaria that the time was come when God *the Father* should no longer be worshipped in a particular place, but *everywhere*:—"The hour cometh when ye shall neither in this mountain, nor yet at Jerusalem, worship *the Father*. But the hour cometh, and now is, when the true worshippers shall worship the Father in spirit and in truth: for the Father seeketh such to worship him."* How can we worship God the Father *everywhere*, if he be not everywhere *present* to receive our worship? Again: *God the Son* says, "Where two or three are gathered together in my name, *there am I in the midst of them*."† Though in a thousand different places at the same moment two or three are gathered together in my name, yet, *wherever* they are so gathered, in *each* of those places am I in *the midst of them*. And yet we are to believe that "God the Son cannot be even in two places at the same instant!" Of course in his *human* nature he cannot, but in his *divine* nature he both can be and *is everywhere present*. He saw Nathanael when he was under the fig tree;‡ and he declared of himself that he was *in heaven*, at the very time he was talking to Nicodemus upon earth.§ To deny omnipresence to any person of the Godhead, is to deny that he is God. For of every Person it is true: "Am I a God at hand, saith the Lord, and not a God afar off? Can any hide himself in secret places that I cannot see him? saith

---

* John iv. 21, 23. † Matt. xviii. 19, 20. ‡ John i. 48—50.
§ John iii. 13.

the Lord. Do not I fill heaven and earth? saith the Lord."*

2. Again: The Mormonite doctrine of *Faith* is false and unscriptural.

(i.) The author of the "Lectures on Faith," having quoted the words, "Through faith we understand that the worlds were framed by the word of God, so that things which are seen were not made of things which do appear," adds this comment upon them:—

"By this we understand that the principle of power which existed in the bosom of God, by which the worlds were framed, was faith; and that it is by reason of this principle of power existing in the Deity that all created things exist.........Take this principle or attribute—for it is an attribute—from the Deity, and he would cease to exist."‡

Really it is almost waste of words to argue about such barefaced, and, we must add, childish perversions as this. St. Paul had said, in Heb. xi. v. 1—"Faith is the substance of things hoped for, *the evidence of things not seen*." Here is not a syllable about its being a "principle of power;" but an "evidence of things not seen." And then he gives an example: How do we understand that the worlds were framed? We did not see them framed: their creation is one of the "things not seen," of which *faith* is the *evidence*; for "through faith we understand that they were framed. It was by the "*word*," not the *faith*, of God that they were framed. "By the *word* of the Lord were the heavens made, and all the host of them by the breath of his mouth."§ The monstrous notion of "faith existing in God" is contrary alike to reason and revelation. Faith necessarily supposes *imperfection* in the party exercising it. We do not want to *believe* what we *see* and *know*. God sees and knows, and is perfectly acquainted with everything, therefore

---

* Jerem. xxiii. 23, 24. See also Ps. cxxxix.; 1 Kings viii. 27.
† Heb. xi. 3.
‡ Book of Covenants, p. 3; where much more to the same effect may be found. § Ps. xxxiii. 6.

he can have no need of faith. It is a thing for creatures, not for the Creator. It is the substance of things *hoped for;* but how can God *hope for* anything? It is the evidence of things *not seen;* but what is there that is *not seen* to him? "All things are naked and opened unto the eyes of him with whom we have to do."*

(ii.) But their doctrine of faith as exercised by *man* is also false. In the "Lectures" it is distinctly stated that we *obtain* faith "*through*," or by means of, "the sacrifice of all earthly things." Thus, for instance, we are told:—

"It is in vain for persons to fancy to themselves that they are heirs with those, or can be heirs with them, who have offered their all in sacrifice, *and by this means obtained faith in God and favour with him, so as to obtain eternal life, unless,*" &c.

Again:—

"But those who do not make the sacrifice cannot enjoy this faith, because men *are dependent upon this sacrifice in order to obtain this faith*," &c.

Now here, we say, is a great and vital error, and that in a systematic course of lectures on the subject of faith intended for "students." The Gospel of Christ does, indeed, require us to sacrifice, or be ready to sacrifice, all earthly things.† But this sacrifice, like all other good works, is the *fruit,* not the *procuring cause,* of faith. It is produced by faith; not faith "*obtained*" by it. "Faith worketh by love." He who believes in Christ loves Christ, and therefore is ready to sacrifice all for Christ. It was by faith that Moses refused "the treasures in Egypt;" not by refusing them that he obtained faith.‡ Holy Scripture expressly declares that faith, so far from being obtained by any such sacrifice, is "*the gift of God.*" "By grace are ye saved through faith; and that not of yourselves: it is the gift of God."§ "Unto you *it is given* in the be-

---

* Heb. iv. 13.   † Luke xiv. 25—33.   ‡ Heb. xi. 24—6.
§ Eph. ii. 8.

D

half of Christ, not only to believe on him, but also to suffer for his sake."* Once more, we ask, shall it be, Mormonism or the Bible? The two cannot stand together. They are at deadly enmity.

(iii.) We will conclude with a few words on that all-important point to every dying sinner—*the way of obtaining salvation.* Here, alas! Mormonite teachers are again in fatal error. We have before us the 2nd part of the "Kingdom of God," which treats of "the nature and character of the laws of adoption, or the invariable rule by which aliens are admitted into the kingdom of God as citizens;" or, in other words, since "salvation is only to be obtained in the kingdom of God," the tract in question professes to tell us how we must be saved. Four requisites are named—Faith, Repentance, Baptism, and Laying on of Hands. Now in the general scheme we remark:

1. First, That *man's state by nature is overlooked.* With regard to infants, we are told that they are *without sin!* "Sin is the transgression of a law." Infants have transgressed no law, and, therefore, they are without sin. Baptism is FOR THE REMISSION OF SINS; but infants have no sins to be remitted, therefore they need no baptism." Here is no distinction drawn between *original* and *actual* sin; but a slurring over, if not an absolute denial, of the truth, that we are "*by nature the children of wrath;*"† and have every one of us to say with David, "Behold, I was shapen in iniquity; and in sin did my mother conceive me."‡ Then again, we are told to believe and repent; but these actions, so far as anything is said about them, are described as being quite within our own power; whereas, it is no more possible for man *of himself* to believe savingly and repent truly, than it is for him to keep the law of God perfectly. The Bible says we are "*dead* in trespasses and sins," and as a *dead* man cannot repent and believe, we

---

* Philip. i. 29. † Eph. ii. 3. ‡ Ps. li. 5.

must be *quickened*" before we can do either.* The Bible says that faith is "*the gift of God.*" The Bible tells of him who is exalted " to be a prince and a Saviour, for *to give repentance* to Israel, and forgiveness of sins."† Mr. Orson Pratt, on the other hand, while he allows that "abstract faith alone can benefit no being," declares of *saving faith*,—the faith, for instance, of the three thousand who were converted on the day of Pentecost,—that it "was founded wholly upon the evidences then set before them;" that "the faith they had in this fact was not different from the faith they had in any other fact; and that "the faith that Jesus is the Son of God, is the same as the faith that Solomon is the Son of David; faith in both of these facts *coming by evidence, and in no other way.*" We do not mean to undervalue evidence, but we do assert, that the faith that Jesus is the Son of God—if it be a *saving* faith—is NOT *the same* as the faith that Solomon is the Son of David. The latter is a mere act of the mind, the former affects the *heart;* for "with *the heart* man believeth unto righteousness." Neither does saving faith come by evidence, *and in no other way,* for, as we have said more than once, "*it is the gift of God.*" It can only be produced in the heart by the Almighty power of God, the Holy Ghost.

(ii.) And this brings us to another point. *The work of the Holy Spirit is disregarded.* We hear much of the miraculous gifts of the Holy Ghost, but little or nothing of his quickening, renewing, sanctifying grace. The first great want of the truly awakened sinner is thus left unacknowledged and unprovided for. Tell him to repent and believe, and he will answer, I would, but I *cannot.* The Saviour and the Saviour's Gospel comfort him with this reply, "Ask, and ye shall have; seek, and ye shall find; knock, and it shall be opened unto you. Your heavenly Father will give the Holy Spirit to them that ask him."‡ But Mormonism

* Eph. ii. 1—10.   † Acts. v. 31.   ‡ Luke xi. 9—13.

bids him believe, repent, be baptized, first; and then "next, seek after the gift of the Holy Ghost." But what gift? The power of working miracles, and speaking with tongues and the like—things which cannot be proved to be necessary to salvation by a single passage of Scripture—not the absolutely necessary gift of his grace in the heart. "If any man," says St. Paul, "have not the Spirit of Christ, he is none of his." But how is the possession of the Spirit of Christ manifested? By working miracles? By speaking with tongues? By prophesying? No! but by "being spiritually minded," by having spiritual life, by "mortifying the deeds of the body," and "possessing the spirit of adoption."*

(iii.) *Baptism is unduly exalted.* There is but little said about baptism in the New Testament, and St. Paul seems to speak even disparagingly of it as compared with preaching. "Christ sent me not to baptise, but to preach the Gospel."† But Mormonism—here, as ever, opposite to Scripture—exalts baptism above measure. I believe that "the promise of forgiveness of sins is visibly signed and sealed" in baptism, but I dare not say with Mr. Orson Pratt, "Baptism is not, as many false teachers now affirm, '*an outward sign of an inward grace;*' but it is an ordinance *whereby* a believing penitent sinner *obtains a forgiveness* of all past sins;" for Scripture nowhere says so. I believe that baptism is "generally necessary to salvation;" but I cannot say that it is "the condition of salvation," and "as much essential to salvation as faith or repentance;" because the Bible would not bear me out. I find forgiveness of sins and salvation promised to faith alone, but never to baptism alone.‡

(iv.) *The Glory of Christ is obscured.* "Not holding the head," is the fatal mistake of all heresy.

* Rom. viii. 6, 9, 10, 13, 15.   † 1 Cor. i. 17.
‡ John iii. 16, 18, 36; Acts xiii. 38, 9.

In the system of Mormonism the atonement of Christ is acknowledged, but it is very little dwelt upon, while his *mediation* and *intercession* are hardly named. These grand fundamental truths are not brought prominently forward. The sinner is not urged, entreated, besought, as he loves his soul, to lay hold of them and make them his own. Christ is not made the sun and centre of their system,—Christ in the glory of his Person as the God-man,—in the perfection of his atoning sacrifice,—in all his offices as our Mediator and Redeemer;—our Prophet, Priest, and King, is not set clearly before perishing sinners as their only hope—their one, all-sufficient refuge and deliverer. There is no being determined to " know nothing, save Jesus Christ and him crucified :"—no proclaiming " the unsearchable riches of Christ." This alone is sufficient to stamp Mormonism as a soul-destroying heresy. Anything that hides Christ,—anything that comes between him and the soul,—anything that dares to obscure his glory—is not of God, and must be at once rejected with abhorrence. Once more, then, Shall it be Mormonism or the Bible? Mormonism without Christ? or the Bible with Christ? Mormonism without salvation? or the Bible with salvation?

And now, dear Reader, whoever you are, I have a brief word for you before we part.

1. *Are you a Mormonite, or in danger of becoming one?* I have spoken severely of your system, and you are inclined perhaps to regard me as your enemy. I am *its* enemy—its sworn enemy, for it is the enemy of God, and of his truth. But I am *your friend*. Believe me I have spoken, and do speak in love to your soul. My prayer is that this little tract may be the means of saving some of you. Read it as the message of one who wishes you well,—as the faithful reproof of a friend. Are you in *earnest* about your soul? Are you *heartily* seeking salvation? Oh! beware of trifling

in these things. Mormonism deals with *religion*—with *the way to be saved*. It is a matter of life and death—the life or death of your precious soul. *Why* are you prepared to take up with Mormonism? Because there are some things in it which *suit* and *please* you? because you look *to get some worldly good* by it? because your friends persuade you? because you think it a fine thing to be promised direct revelations from heaven, and the power of working miracles? because you like *to be somebody?* Tell me, Are any or all these things worth *risking your soul for?* Here then is my advice to you—Take down your Bible, turn to Luke xi. 13, kneel down, and ask God, in Christ's name, to fulfil the promise there made to you—to teach you by his Holy Spirit *the true way to be saved*. Read through this tract, turning to the texts in your Bible, and pray God to shew you by the same Spirit whether Mormonism is or is not opposed to the Bible. And then when you find, as you will find, that *it is* awfully opposed to the Bible, ask yourself, Which shall I take, Mormonism or the Bible? May God give you grace to make the right choice, to take the Bible with its precious Saviour, its full and free salvation, and to renounce Mormonism and all other inventions of men once and for ever!

2. Lastly, Reader, *Are you* NOT *a Mormonite?* No; no fear of that, perhaps you say. Well, " be not high-minded, but fear." " Let him that thinketh he standeth, take heed lest he fall." The fact that so many thousands are led away by such a system as Mormonism, should teach us what human nature is,—should make us tremble for ourselves,—should lead us earnestly to pray under a sense of our own helplessness: " Hold up my goings in thy paths, that my footsteps slip not."* Two cautions let me add. First, *Beware of idle curiosity.* Do not read Mormonite books, or attend Mormonite meetings, or talk with

---

* Ps. xvii. 5.

Mormonites, just that you may know what they hold. The system is false and wicked: have nothing to do with it. Pray for and pity Mormonites, but do not listen to their arguments or read their books. "If there come any unto you, and bring not this doctrine, (the doctrine of Christ,) receive him not into your house, neither bid him God speed: For he that biddeth him God speed is partaker of his evil deeds."* Secondly, *Beware of resting in right notions and a correct creed.* It is a great thing to have a clear head knowledge of the truth as it is in Jesus. But it is not enough. It will not *surely* keep you from error in any days,—much less in these days,—when error abounds. And, if it could, it will not save your soul. True, spiritual religion—the religion of the *heart*, and not of the *head* only—is what we all want. That, and that alone, will, by God's grace, keep us through life, support us in death, and bring us safe to heaven.

* 2 John 10, 11.

NOTE A.

The following is extracted from the *"Times" Newspaper* of January 20th, 1852.

"MORMONISM.—*The New York National Police Gazette* contains a mass of disgusting details relative to the proceedings of this sect at the Salt Lake. A correspondent of that paper, writing from Utah, says : 'The pluralist wife system is in full vogue here. Governor Young is said to have ninety wives. He drove along the streets a few days ago with sixteen of them in a long carriage, fourteen of them having each an infant at her breast. It is said Heber C. Kimball, one of the Triune Council, and the second person in the Trinity, has almost an equal number, and among them are a mother and her two daughters. Each man can have as many wives as he can maintain; that is after the women have been picked and culled by the head men. Whole pages might be filled with the surprising and disgusting details of the state of affairs here.' It is a lamentable fact that, at the present time, numbers of people are leaving Great Britian to join the Mormons, notwithstanding the disclosures that are so constantly being made."

NOTE B.

The flagrant ignorance displayed in the above comment is yet more apparent when we notice that the words " of one that hath a familar spirit " are the translation of a *single word* in the Hebrew; and that wherever the expression "familiar spirit" occurs in the English version, there is only a *substantive* in the Hebrew. The adjective "familiar" therefore is, strictly speaking, a mere addition of the translators, to express the kind of intercourse that subsists between the spirit and the person consulting it. So much for Mr. Pratt's unfortunate criticism !

DIXON, MARKET STREET, CAMBRIDGE.

MORMONISM.

A NUMEROUS sect has arisen in America who style themselves "Latter Day Saints," and are called by others Mormonites. The term Mormonites is taken from the book entitled "The Book of Mormon." The design of this tract is to give a plain account, *first*, of the beginning and progress of the religion of Jesus Christ, and, *then*, of the religion of the Latter Day Saints or Mormonites; that the reader may compare them together, and judge for himself whether Mormonism have any claims to be received in addition to the Bible as a religion from God. We shall take our account of Christianity from the New Testament, and our account of Mormonism from the acknowledged writings of the party. Our object is to state the simple truth.

The conviction which we have is very strong that Mormonism is a delusion, and that no person can be misled by it who is well grounded in the history and doctrines of the gospel. We, at the same time, know that many persons have received erroneous notions respecting the character and life of Joseph Smith, the founder of Mormonism; and that not a few of his followers imagine that the doctrines which he taught were revealed to him from Heaven, without *weighing the kind of proof he offered that it was so, with the kind of proof we have for the Divine authority of the Holy Scriptures.*

As Mormonites acknowledge the Divine authority of the Bible, we wish to show that they are right in so doing, by giving the *proofs* of that authority. But, as all the reasons which prove that the Bible is of God, also prove that *all*

THE RELIGIOUS TRACT SOCIETY, INSTITUTED 1799.
56, PATERNOSTER ROW, AND 65, ST. PAUL'S CHURCHYARD.

other books pretending to be from him are only the works of men, we feel it to be our duty as Christians to make this proof as plain as we can. We do not intend to draw a caricature of Mormonism, or to treat either its founder or his followers with rudeness. Various opinions will be formed of their social and political conduct as American citizens, and of the worldly advantages which are held out to induce persons in this country to emigrate for the purpose of joining them. Our present concern is not with any of these things. We are going to deal only with what we regard as their errors on *religious* subjects, and the evil effects of such errors.

Jesus Christ appeared among men at a time when the whole civilized world was under the government of the Romans. Judea, the country in which he lived, was a conquered province of the Roman empire. The people of that country had been favoured with a religion ordained by God; and their sacred Scriptures, held by them in veneration as the word of God, recorded God's dealings with their fathers, and contained many prophecies to be fulfilled in later times. Among these prophecies were those which promised a Prophet like unto Moses—a Priest after the order of Melchizedec—and a King more glorious than Solomon and David, who should rule the world in righteousness. Jesus of Nazareth declared himself to be that Prophet. His apostles proclaimed him as that Priest, and demanded homage to him as that King. All this was *proved*.

How was it proved?

First. That Jesus was the *Prophet, Priest, and King,* foretold by the ancient prophets, was proved by showing that *there was no other person* to whom the descriptions of the prophets could be applied. Before the appearance of Jesus there had never been a person born at Bethlehem, of the family of David, who taught the people, opened the eyes of the blind, was rejected, put to death, "as an offering for sin," raised from the dead, and seated at the right hand of God. There was no one person, up to that time, of whom these things could be said. Nor was it pretended, at that time, that any such person had appeared in Judea.

Secondly. It was proved by plain facts that *these descriptions did apply to Jesus.* The *public registers* proved that he was of the family of David, and that he was born at Bethlehem. The people in Galilee, in Judea, and at Jerusalem, *knew* quite well that he went from place to place teaching and working miracles. His death was *public*. The Jews charged him with blasphemy because he said he was the Son of God; and he confessed to Pilate that he was a king. There were hundreds of persons who saw him alive after his death, and who were so sure of this *plain fact* that they were ready to lay down their lives in upholding it. A company of these witnesses had followed him daily for three or four years. One of them, who sold him to his enemies, was so stung with remorse for what he had done that he brought back the money he had received for delivering him, saying he had betrayed innocent blood; and he went and hanged himself. The eleven men whom Jesus chose as his witnesses, were enabled to speak foreign languages *which they had never learned;* to heal sick persons; to raise the dead; and to teach truths which had never entered into the minds of men. The testimony of these *witnesses* is preserved in the books of the New Testament. The account of the life, death, and resurrection of Jesus was made public by these witnesses within a few days after his ascension, in the places where he had lived and died, and where they appealed to thousands of people—who were *not* his followers—in proof that what they said was true.

Now, all these things being true, as Mormonites acknowledge no less than others professing to be Christians, there is no difficulty in giving a straightforward account of the beginning of our religion. The account was given to enemies as well as to friends. It was given first in Judea, and then in almost every part of the Roman empire. It was so clear and so convincing to many thousands of people in different countries that they received it, acted upon it, and became altogether new men. They left the religions in which they had been brought up. They bore persecution. They endured meekly the opposition of friends, neighbours, priests, and magistrates. By their constancy and perseverance they changed the whole face of society. At length they overturned idolatry, and many of the vices which idolatry encourages, throughout the civilized world. All this was done by truth, goodness, suffering, by the power of the Spirit of God in the hearts of men, without any force, without any worldly influence, but *against* force, and against worldly influence of every kind. Here was the fulfilment of the ancient prophecies. Here was the proof that what Jesus and his apostles taught was true. There is no other way of explaining how it came to pass that such a religion as the religion of Jesus Christ could have got a footing in the world.

Thirdly. The *character* of Jesus, which is given by his disciples, and confirmed by the admissions or the silence of his enemies, is the *most natural, lovely, and majestic* in the history of mankind,—the only one of which we have the assurance that it is *faultless*. It is exceedingly important to remember that these disciples never praise Jesus in their account of his life, never express admiration or wonder. All they do is to tell us some facts :—what he did, and what he taught, and how he suffered, and died, and rose, and went to heaven. We seem to see him, to hear him, for ourselves. Everything is just as it ought to be: he always says the thing that is true and wise; and, like himself, his *works* are open and simple, without any parade or pretence. There is no appearance of art, nothing that could suggest the notion of trick, concealment, or imposture. So wise a teacher, so calm, so practical, could not have been self-deceived. So perfectly holy and benevolent a heart cannot be suspected of even the thought of deceiving others. We should as soon think of the laws of nature being delusions as the teachings of Jesus Christ. People who read the New Testament must become acquainted with the character of Jesus Christ in a way which fills them with reverence and love, if they *reflect on what they read so as to feel its power upon their hearts*. It is very remarkable that in whatever country men live, or at whatever period of time, the more they study the New Testament the more they see of the singular beauty, the engaging loveliness, the sublime majesty, the living completeness of the character of our Saviour. He does not belong only to one age, or to one country. He is of all times and of all lands. He is "The Man." In him we see a perfect man; what God would have every man to be; what every man ought to be; what the religion of Christ is designed to make men;—what men will be when the purpose for which the Son of God became man shall be accomplished in them.

Fourthly. The *reason* why Jesus suffered and died

according to the history contained in the Gospels, is one which *fully agrees with the truth* of that history. This reason was partly made known in the Old Testament Scriptures, by typical sacrifices, and by strong expressions used in some of the prophecies. To this reason John the Baptist referred when he saw Jesus walking, and said, " Behold the Lamb of God, which taketh away the sin of the world," John i. 29. See 1 John iii. 5; 1 Pet. iii. 18; 2 Cor. v. 21; 1 John i. 7. This was the great truth which Jesus himself taught in his discourse with Nicodemus; in his addresses to the Jews at Jerusalem; and in his parting words to his disciples before his death. The preaching of the apostles held Jesus forth as THE SAVIOUR. They spoke and wrote of him as reconciling men to God by his death—saving them by his life—dying for their sins—rising for their justification—appearing for them before God—giving them redemption by his blood, through the remission of their sins. All that Jesus was, did, suffered—and still is, and does—is held forth as the plea on which men who confess their sins ask to be forgiven. It is *for his sake* that we are pardoned, accepted, justified, made children of God, and prepared for heaven. When we read the Gospels in this light, we see how unspeakably important to us it is that He who came to be our Saviour should be so perfect as we find he was. We, also, see what a glorious work that must be for which *such* a Saviour was sent into the world. A *wise* man might have saved us from *ignorance*. A *strong* man might have saved some from *bodily* evils. A *good* man might have saved others from much *sorrow*. But who could save men from their *sins*? Who could make it right for God to pardon sinners? Who could bring them to God—humbled, renewed in his own likeness, and fitted for his kingdom? It is only when we keep in mind this peculiarity of the gospel that we are rightly impressed with the immeasurable difference between Jesus Christ and all other beings. " Was Paul crucified for you?" Jesus *was* crucified for us. His being crucified for us was the crowning act of his love. Here lies the strength of his claim upon us. Our obligation to him is unlike our obligation to any other. We owe ourselves to him. We are to live to him. We are to be jealous for his honour. We are to regard our being as bound up with the assertion of his Divine and sole right over us as our only Saviour. Our religion is not a mere belief of history, or a mere holding of doctrine. It sways our hearts. It makes us grateful, loyal, and devoted, to the Son of God. It is His truth that we venerate. His will becomes our law. His sacrifice is not more our pledge of peace than it is our motive to obedience. We see in his spotless character the mirror of God—the righteousness which justifies—the model which requires, urges, and encourages our imitation. Thus Jesus Christ *is* the Christian religion— its founder, its object, its glory, its life, its aim; as an apostle says, "For to me to live is Christ"—Christ is our life—" I live by the faith of the Son of God, who loved me, and gave himself for me," Gal. ii. 20.

Fifthly. The *commission* which Jesus gave to his apostles was *to bear witness to his resurrection from the dead* as the Son of God, and the Saviour of men. The Jews denied that he was the Son of God. His resurrection *proved* that he *was*. That a man who had been publicly put to death should be seen alive after his death, so that those who knew him best should be sure that it was he, and should receive instructions from him for doing the work which he gave them to do, was a most wonderful thing. But *there* were the witnesses—at the time, and the place of his death—declaring that they had seen him, and by their extraordinary wisdom, and extraordinary power, *proving* that they were not deceived nor deceivers, but intelligent, calm, sincere, and faithful men. These men could not be deceived in so plain a matter as this—namely, that they were conversing with one whom they had known for years. Nor could they be deceivers:—for they had nothing to gain, and every thing to lose, by declaring what they did declare, if it were not true. We must remember the circumstances in which Jesus rose from the dead, if we would understand the importance of this fact. And we must remember the circumstances of the witnesses, if we would see how true it is that they had seen him alive after his crucifixion. We know that Jesus had foretold his resurrection; that he offered this fact as the sign that he was the Son of God; that he was put to death because he was charged with blasphemy for saying this; that the Jews obtained a guard to watch the sepulchre in which his dead body was laid, besides sealing the stone; that on the third day they could not find his body, but got up a silly story about his disciples having stolen it; and that there were many intelligent, sober, and truly pious men who declared in the plainest and most public manner that they had *seen him alive;* and that these men *proved* by their teaching, their lives, and their miracles, that he had fulfilled his promise to endow them with power from on high. Now there is nothing at all like this in the whole history of mankind.

Sixthly. Great *numbers* of people at the time *believed* what these witnesses declared and taught, and *became the avowed followers* of Christ. By becoming followers of Christ they made known their belief of the gospel, of its facts, of its doctrines, of its Divine authority, and of its spiritual power in their own experience. They exposed themselves to almost every kind of sacrifice and trouble, by becoming Christians. *They did not defend themselves by force against their persecutors. They did not breathe revenge against them. They never formed a political body.* They had nothing visible, nothing that could be handled, nothing that the world values, in consequence of their believing the gospel. On the contrary, many of them were cruelly used, not a few were put in prison, and some were even put to death, for no other reason than what their enemies called their obstinacy in holding fast their religion; all this is simply told us in the Acts of the Apostles, and in the letters which were written by Peter and by Paul to Christians in several parts of the world. This is all very natural:—natural that people believing what *they* believed should live as they did; and natural that their enemies, feeling as we know the enemies of true religion feel, should have treated them as they did. But it is *not* natural that men should believe what these Christians believed without having *proof* that it was true. We know that they had that proof. We are plainly told what it was. They had the testimony of sensible and honest men, and the testimony of their own experience. Everything was *above board*, as we say: "This thing was not done in a corner." They knew very well whether they heard, saw, felt, the things of which we read. And we know, that *if they had not*, such a book as the New Testament was impossible. Only think of a person writing to people in London or Liverpool, as people who had suffered persecution, and who had witnessed miracles, and who had been turned from sin to holiness; while those people knew all the time, that they had *not* been persecuted, had *not* seen miracles, had *not* been spiritually converted; and then, if you can, imagine it possible that such letters as the Epistles in the New Testament, should be received by wise and good men as inspired by the Holy Spirit! You feel at once, that such suppositions are mere nonsense.

Seventhly. Ever since the death of the apostles, *the Bible*, containing the Old and New Testaments, *has been read* in Christian churches *as the written word* of God. This is matter of history. No professing Christian doubts it. No unbeliever has ever disproved it. The Bible is read at the present day. No one can explain, in any other way, how the Bible *began* to be so read. This is a very simple, natural, and straightforward account of the matter. It is the only historical account of it in existence. There is no reason whatever why any one should hesitate to receive it as true. It is not the invention of Protestants; for the Roman Catholics give the same account. It is not a modern invention; the history is older than the history of England. It is not questioned by Mormonites. Well, then, if the Bible has been *rightly received as the word* of God from the beginning of the Christian era, it is reasonable to ask—whether we are wise, right, safe, religious, *in adding any other book* to it? Does the Bible itself lead us to look for any other book? Does it say anything about pretenders to inspiration? Does it give us any directions about dealing with such pretenders? Have there been such pretenders? What have they been, what have they done, what has become of them, and of their pretensions? In answer to these proper and pertinent questions, let the following plain facts be well considered:—

I. The Bible, including the Old and New Testaments, *does not lead us to expect any other book, or writings, or messages* inspired of God. The witnesses of Christ have left their testimony in the New Testament; and the New Testament proves the Divine authority of the Old Testament. There is no occasion for any further witnesses. We may here know all that needs to be known. The way to worship God, to approach him for salvation, to please him by a holy life, is as plain as possible. The character of God, his promises, his commandments, his revelation of a future judgment and of an eternal state of happiness or misery, are given in clear words, fully, strongly, and repeatedly. Moses and the prophets foretold a future Teacher. Jesus gave his Holy Spirit to the apostles. The apostles did their work, and left the gospel in the churches for the instruction of all nations and all ages. They did not foretell, as the ancient prophets had foretold, that there would be a *new* prophet, an *additional* revelation, *another* Bible.

II. The apostles *did foretell* that there *would be pretenders to inspiration*, boasting teachers, false prophets. Examine the following passages: Acts xx. 29, 30; Gal. i. 8, 9; 2 Thess. ii. 1—12; 1 Tim. iv. 1; vi. 3, 5; 2 Tim. iii. 1—5; iv. 3, 4; Titus i. 10, 11; James i. 21—26; iii. 13—18; 1 Pet. iv. 11; 2 Pet. ii. 1, 17—19; iii. 1—3; 1 John ii. 18, 19, 24—27; iv. 1; Jude 17—23; Rev. xxii. 18, 19.

From the solemn and earnest warnings of the inspired writers it is manifest that there has been at all times, and that there will still continue to be, a danger of forgetting and neglecting the lessons of the Bible, and of being led away by human weakness and sinfulness to fearful delusions. We know what the speculative curiosity of men desires. We see how easy it is for some to be carried away by the opinions, the assertions, the promises, or the pretensions of their fellow-men. We are put on our guard. We are exhorted to stand fast by the old truth which was taught by the apostles. We are expressly told that there will be "false prophets," "false teachers," "seducers." We are commanded to *try* all pretensions by the standard which God has given us in his holy word. We are warned against the indulgence of those feelings which would prompt us to deceive, or make us ready to be deceived, in these sacred and momentous affairs. We cannot deny the Divine authority of these fore-warnings. We perceive in them the proofs of the wisdom of God. They are the words of his faithful love. It is part of our practical religion as Christians, to take heed to ourselves. We are to watch and to pray that we may not enter into temptation. *Fore-warned is fore-armed.* Let men keep firm hold of the words which they have been taught from Heaven, and which have been so graciously preserved for their learning. Let them settle it in their minds, that *every pretence to authority* like that which belongs to the Bible is to be at once rejected, *and rejected for this very reason*. If a man's mind is not settled on this point, he is sure to be the prey of the first deceiver that has the power to mislead him. The importance of being decided in such a case is very plain. We do not know that anything can be plainer. Since Jesus Christ has been proved to be the Son of God, and both he and his apostles tell us in the strongest words that deceivers will arise, there is every ground for suspecting the intelligence, or the honesty, of any man who declares to us that he has received a revelation from God. On this clear and simple ground we refuse to have any thing to do with Mormonism. It cannot be received instead of the Bible. It ought not to be put *on a level with the Bible*. The latest writers of the Bible, foreseeing that things of this kind would arise, have plainly told us what to do. If Mormonism has any explanations to give of any part of the Bible, let those explanations be treated, as all human explanations must be treated, according to their worth. If they agree with the plain meaning of the words of our Lord Jesus Christ and his apostles, and promote the manifest design of the whole Bible, they will be received by candid Christians with thankfulness; but if men pretend that they come to us with Divine authority, with the same authority as the Old and New Testaments, it is our duty, and for our safety, to cast them away as worse than worthless, for " no lie is of the truth," 1 John ii. 21. If the people of America, England, and other countries, who have become Mormonites, had valued their Bibles as all Christians profess to value them, and if they had used their Bibles as Christ and his apostles have taught us to use them, the pretensions of Joseph Smith would have been condemned *at once*. But he knew, as is too well known, that multitudes bear the Christian name who are *not* thus prepared to resist imposture. And he knew, too, that there is something very exciting in a new religion—especially if its teachers are loud and fierce in condemning others, and still more if advantages of a worldly nature are held out to induce the *poor*, the *enterprising*, the *discontented*, or the *disappointed*, to become disciples.

Now it cannot be denied that there must be a great deal of error among the many sects that profess the Christian religion, and that people are sometimes greatly perplexed when they want to know who is right and who is wrong, to understand what is the truth, and what is error in religion. Neither can it be denied that in all sects persons may be found whose lives are far from being what they ought to be. Let all this be granted. What then? Does it follow that there is no truth held in common by all sects? Does it follow that they are *all wrong in every particular?* Have there not always been, and are there not now, great numbers of humble and pious men and women worshipping God according to their views of his will, through faith in the one Saviour? Do not such persons form the church of Christ, by whatever name they may be called, and even though they may be erroneously taught on matters that do not prevent their sole trust in Christ, and their practical holiness? If they are in error, it is an error in *their* understanding of particular parts of Scripture, not in the Scripture *itself*; but it is to the Scriptures, and not to human forms of belief, that we are to go for direction in all such matters. Surely he who takes the Bible for his guide, and follows its plain teaching, will learn the way of salvation, and the path of duty, and the source to which he may calmly look for comfort in this life, and for eternal joy in the life to come! Even if we were to take the gloomiest view of the mistakes and the faults of people professing to be Christians, how can that prove that we need a *new revelation?*

We know, from the surest evidence, tnat the apostles of our Lord were commissioned to teach men the way of salvation. And we know that, by signs and wonders and divers miracles and gifts of the Holy Ghost, God bare witness to their message. These signs and wonders were numerous, various, and important. They are matters of history. The history has been tried by every test by which men try history, and it has been *proved* to be true. All who believe the doctrines, and act on the directions of these inspired messengers, have a proof *within themselves* that in this affair there is no imposture or delusion. The doctrines of the gospel are the manifestations of the wisdom of God, imparted by the Holy Spirit. The apostles were inspired. To them, and by them, the word of truth was revealed. They had "the mind of Christ." They spoke and wrote the "wisdom of God in a mystery." They had "a mouth and wisdom" given them by Christ. They received "the Spirit which is of God," and "the deep things of God," which "the Spirit searcheth," they declared in the words which the "Holy Ghost teacheth." (See John xx. 21, 22; 1 Cor. ii. 7, 10, 12, 13, 16; John xiv. 26; xv. 26, 27; xvi. 13, 14; Gal. i. 11, 12; 1 Thess. ii. 13; 2 Peter iii. 15.) Various gifts were imparted to the apostles, and to those on whom the apostles laid their hands for that purpose. (Acts viii. 14—19; x. 44; xix. 6; Rom. i. 11; 1 Cor. ix. 1, 2; 2 Cor. xi. 4, 5.) These were the "signs of an apostle." They were intended to prove that the apostles were indeed the witnesses of the risen and ascended Saviour, to fit them for the work of declaring the message of God, and to secure the preservation of that message to all ages and all nations. The men of every time and place need to be taught the things of God, and to be guided to salvation. All who receive the truth in "the love of the truth," *are* thus taught and guided. What the apostles taught is recorded, for universal and constant use, in their writings. We believe their words for the same reason for which they were believed at first. What we have in the Bible, then, is this:—*The apostolic teaching as written by men who were proved to be commissioned by Christ, and inspired by the Holy Ghost*. The apostles are still the *witnesses* of Christ " to the uttermost parts of the earth." The men are dead: the testimony remains to this day. The tongues are silenced, the hands of the writers are mouldered into dust: the words they uttered and wrote still live. "All flesh is as grass, and all the glory of man as the flower of grass. The grass withereth, and the flower thereof falleth away: but *the word of the Lord endureth for ever*. And this is the word which by the gospel is preached unto you," 1 Pet. i. 24, 25. Now, since our Saviour pronounced a blessing on those who, though they have not seen, yet have believed, he teaches us most forcibly that we are bound to receive the written declaration of those who did see, and who saw *for us* as well as for themselves. However necessary it was to give sensible, visible, tangible proofs of his resurrection to the chosen witnesses, and to accompany their testimony with a body of extraordinary powers befitting their peculiar office, it was "*through their word*" that men were to believe in Christ. This "word" we have. Let us not slight it. Let us not tamper with it. Let us hold it fast, and take heed lest we be deceived by men pretending to have another "word," another revelation It is Christ himself, followed by his inspired servants, who gives us the warning not to be deceived. When any person tells us that he has a revelation from God, he reminds us of the warning. If we believe Christ and his apostles, we shall say, "Jesus I know, and Paul I know; but who are ye?" Acts xix. 15.

III. Notwithstanding the warnings contained in the New Testament, *there have been many pretenders to new revelations* since the days of the apostles. It is clear that there can be no more *witnesses* of the resurrection of Jesus Christ, like the apostles. In this sense, their office died with them, and so did "the signs" of the office. No power was given by Christ to any others at the time when they disappeared from the world, to take their place. If we abide by the Scriptures we feel no want of a new revelation, we find no promise of one, we are taught to reject all professors of this kind.—Among the pretenders to new revelations, who have had many followers, we may mention SIMON MAGUS in the days of the apostles, who founded a sect that bore his name;—MENANDER, who was a follower of Simon;—MONTANUS, in the second century, who gave himself out as the Comforter promised by our Saviour, with a divine commission to complete the precepts of the gospel. He delivered alarming prophecies respecting the Roman empire. His disciples were numerous, and some of them persons of distinction, in Asia, Africa, and some parts of Europe. In the third century, MANES, a Persian, declared himself to be "the Comforter." He established a sect whose opinions continued to excite attention even twelve hundred years after their establishment. All the world knows that MOHAMMED, the false prophet of Arabia, in the seventh century, delivered the *Koran* as a revelation from God, and that this pretended revelation is received by millions of people in Asia, Africa, and some parts of Europe till this day; though it is rejected by all Christians as a mere delusion, contrary to the Bible, and entirely without the *kind* of proofs by which we know the Bible to be from God.

To come nearer to our own times, and to our own country. In 1794, RICHARD BROTHERS published a book called, "A Revealed Knowledge of the Prophecies and Times," of which he said, "It is from visions and revelations, and through the Holy Ghost, that I write this book for the benefit of all men; therefore to say it is false, that I am mad, and an impostor, have a devil, or am out of my senses, constitutes the dangerous sin of blasphemy." He delivered his prophecies before the house of commons. He was put in prison for prophesying that the king of England was soon to die, and the monarchy to be abolished, and the crown of the realm to be delivered up to *him*. He not only believed in his own mission, but was followed by persons of respectable character and station. He said the restoration of the Jews was to happen in 1798, when he would himself appear as their chief, and as the ruler of all the nations. Some of his numerous political guesses were correct; but the greater part of them proved to be false.

At the beginning of the present century, JOANNA SOUTHCOTE, from a pretender to inspiration of the name of Sanderson took up the notion that she too was inspired. She published many books which are now forgotten, though they were greedily sought after and eagerly received as revelations at the time, and for many years after. At the age of sixty she prophesied that she should become the mother of the Prince of peace, on the 19th of October, 1814, at midnight. Thousands of people looked for the birth of "the Shiloh" at the time. There was no birth. Within two months she died, after declaring that "if she was deceived, she was, at all events, misled by some spirit, good or bad." For many years some of her deluded followers believed that she had fallen into a trance, from which they expected her to awake; though her body had been opened, and an account of her last illness and death had been published by a physician; while others, seeing the folly of such a notion as that, believed that she would rise from the dead and become the mother of the promised child. This notion of a child being born arose from her fancying herself to be the woman spoken of, as a symbol of something else, in the book of Revelation. To this day there are persons to be found in England who still cling to this absurdity.

In all the cases we have mentioned—Simon, Menander, Manes, Brothers, Southcote, to which many more might be added, there was the *pretence* of revelation, but not the *proof*. There were followers who believed in each of these pretenders, but they believed *without evidence*. All of them have been exploded, because they had no foundation in *fact*. They were either the imaginations of weak enthusiasts, or the tricks of clever impostors, or a mixture of both. In every one of them we learn how necessary, how wise, how gracious were the forewarnings of Christ and his apostles. Their history shows us, as clearly as the day-light displays the fields, and trees, and animals around us, that there is no safety, no wisdom, no real piety, but in keeping firm hold of the Holy Scriptures.

Now, it so happens that there are in America, in England, and in other countries, multitudes of people who, as we have seen of others, are quite ready for being drawn away by persons who profess (sincerely or insincerely as to their own belief) that they have received messages from Heaven. Ignorant people, who do not know what the Bible really *is*, and what it *says*, may easily be led astray. Careless persons, who do not consider that it is the easiest thing in the world to mistake fancy for truth, are not unlikely to give ear to such pretensions, though they have disregarded the Divine and tried teachings of the Bible. Curious people, who want to know more about either God or man, the past or the future, than the Bible teaches, are prepared to be led away by a man who tells them wonderful stories about angels, and visions, and voices from heaven. Besides persons of the kinds now mentioned, there are vast multitudes who are discontented with their social or political circumstances, who, for *that reason*, may soon become the prey of those who hold out the prospect of *bettering their worldly condition*. And those who hold out such prospects are more likely to succeed with a great many by mixing such prospects with strong assertions of authority from God. When all these things are considered, we are not surprised that such a man as JOSEPH SMITH should have set up for a prophet in America, or that he should have drawn after him great numbers of earnest and enthusiastic followers. *There is nothing new in it.* There is nothing about it which cannot be easily explained without believing that he was inspired. We have the writings of men who *were* inspired. These men have taught us to be on the watch. It would have been strange, therefore, if no such persons as Joseph Smith had arisen. It would have been equally strange if he had found no followers, determined to cleave to the man, to his books, or to his system, notwithstanding all the proofs derived from the Bible that all such people are deceivers, if not of themselves, of all who put their trust in them.

There is one thing which it is but fair to notice just here, before we trace the history of Mormonism from the beginning. It is this: MORMONISM IS A SCHEME FOR RAISING MONEY TO BE SPENT BY THE HEADS OF THE SECT IN ESTABLISHING A POLITICAL SOCIETY IN AMERICA. The *religious* part of it, as we shall prove, is easily seen through; but the *worldly* part is very tempting. Let us now see how Mormonism began.

JOSEPH SMITH, junior, the founder of this scheme, was born at Sharon, Windsor county, in the state of Vermont, North America, in 1805. When he was ten years old he removed, with his parents, to Palmyra, in the state of New York. He had very little education. At the age of fifteen he saw—according to his own account—a supernatural light in a grove near his father's house, and then two glorious beings, exactly like each other, who told him that his sins were forgiven—that all the Christians were in error, none of them acknowledged God—and that, at a future time, the truth would be made known to him. After the vision, this youth, who believed that his sins were forgiven, *without any regard to repentance, or faith in the Saviour*, continued to live in sin. Some time after, before he was eighteen years old, he had, as he said, another vision of an angel, who told him that his sins were forgiven, (still without any repentance or faith, according to the gospel,) and that his prayers were heard; that the millennium was at hand, and that he was chosen of God to bring to pass some of his wonderful works. He professed to have learned, by this angel, that the American Indians were a remnant of Israel who had been taught by prophets, whose writings still existed, and that, if he were faithful, he should be employed in laying these sacred writings before the world. Next morning, he says, the angel told him where these records were to be found. Following the directions thus said to have been given, he went to the place. There, he says, he was filled with the Holy Spirit; the angel again appeared and said "Look," and described the records as containing the fulness of the gospel as it was given to the people of that land. It seems that some years elapsed, in which he professed to have received frequent instructions from the angel before he delivered the records to him. These records were engraved on plates which had the appearance of gold, filled with engravings in Egyptian characters, and bound like the leaves of a book, and fastened with three rings running through them all at one edge. Along with the plates were the Urim and Thummim, two crystal stones, set in two rims of a bow, with which, he says, persons in ancient times called Seers received revelations of past, distant, or future events. By means of these stones, Joseph Smith affirmed that he was enabled by the gift and power of God to translate the inscriptions on the plates. As he was a bad writer, he dictated the words of the translation to another person. The part which he translated is THE BOOK OF MORMON.

About six years after this finding of the plates, while Joseph Smith and another person, named Oliver Cowdrey, were employed in translating the book, they declare that John the Baptist came from heaven and ordained them to the priesthood of Aaron, and commanded them to baptize each other. When Smith had baptized Cowdrey, and Cowdrey had baptized Smith, they ordained one another: though Smith says they had both been ordained by John the Baptist!

We shall examine this Book of Mormon in another tract, and proceed with the history.—Besides this book, there is another called "The book of DOCTRINES AND COVENANTS," which we shall examine along with the Book of Mormon. It relates to government, tithing, building cities and temples, allotting lands, education, raising money, and similar worldly matters.—Two years after the ordination of Smith and Cowdrey, Smith professed to have a revelation from Jesus Christ about money. Then he professed to have revelations concerning the building of a house for himself, and providing for all his temporal necessities.

In addition to these pretended revelations, both Smith and his followers professed to cast out devils, and to heal the sick. In 1830, a church was organized at La Fayette, consisting of thirty persons, including all the family of the Smiths. They soon removed to Kirtland, in Ohio. After remaining there a few weeks, Joseph Smith proceeded, with a few companions, to Cincinnati, Louisville, and then to St. Louis, from thence he walked three hundred miles to Independence, in Jackson county, Missouri. There he professed to have a revelation directing him to build a temple, and to gather the saints. On the Sunday after his removal, Smith preached to the Indians in the wilderness, made a few converts, and professed to have a revelation respecting the raising of money for the building of a temple and the purchase of lands. In three weeks he dedicated the spot on which the temple was to stand. In twenty-four days he and his companions reached Kirtland on their return, when Smith became president, and Sidney Rigdon cashier, of a church, a mill, and a bank, *for the express purpose of making money.* For about two years Smith gained many converts by preaching in various parts of the United States. Much opposition, however, was raised against him. He was dragged from his bed by a mob, who tarred and feathered him. Immediately after this outrage he set out with some of his followers for the state of Missouri, where he had before fixed the spot for the temple. At Independence, which was now called Zion, he was received as prophet, and seer, and president of the high-priesthood of the church. By a pretended revelation, a printing-press, a monthly magazine, and a weekly newspaper were established. While the number of his followers in Kirtland was not more than a hundred and fifty, they amounted in Missouri to many hundreds. These Mormonites in the state of Missouri boasted that they would take the whole state to themselves. They thus spread alarm and hostility around them. They were accused of various crimes; and a conspiracy was raised against them; they were also disturbed by jealousies among themselves. Smith took two other persons, Rigdon and Williams, as his equals in the government. They were ordered by a pretended revelation to search for a rich man of strong faith, to pay their debts. A meeting of the county of Jackson was held, in which it was resolved to expel the Mormons from the county. This led to hard fighting on both sides, which ended in the expulsion of the Mormons. For four years they lived in Clay county. Thither Smith repaired with a hundred-and-fifty *armed men.* Though he professed to see visions of angels, and to heal diseases, he could not cure the cholera in his own camp. He appears to have remained only a week in Missouri at that time, and to have returned to Kirtland. But his bank there failed; and he departed in the night once more for Missouri. There were many divisions, and some desertions among his followers. The opposition of their enemies increased. A war was ke up for several weeks. A body of Morm called the "Danite Band," or "Destroying Angels," was organized, who *took an oath to support the heads of the church in all things.* The militia of the state was called out against them. Smith was apprehended on charges of treason, murder, and felony. He escaped from prison; in the mean time his followers were driven from the state of Missouri. In a few months they amounted to fifteen thousand persons, including children, and obtained a settlement in the state of Illinois. There they founded the city of Nauvoo, or Beautiful. Smith became the mayor of this city, and general of the Nauvoo militia. Many of the inhabitants were from England, where, in 1843, their numbers had increased to more than ten thousand. In 1841, Smith had a pretended revelation directing the building of a splendid temple at Nauvoo, to which all the "saints" were to give the tenth of their property, time, or labour. The first stone was laid in April, 1841, with great military pomp, Smith appearing on horseback, and reviewing his legion. His followers in America and in Europe are said to have amounted, about this time, to a hundred and fifty thousand, of whom there were nearly thirty thousand in the territories near Nauvoo. Joseph Smith was now in his glory. In 1844 he offered himself as candidate for the presidency of the United States. He had many wives, as had also Rigdon. This "spiritual wife" system involved him in great trouble and disgrace. For forcibly destroying the property of a party excommunicated on account of their exposure of this system, he was served with a warrant from an officer of the government. Smith denied the authority of the warrant, and ordered the marshal of Nauvoo to drive the constable who delivered it from the city. The militia of the county was called out. The Mormons fortified their city. The governor of the state of Illinois took the field and persuaded the Mormons to submit to the law, and promised to protect them. While Smith lay in prison at Carthage to take his trial, a writ was served upon him for high treason against the state of Illinois.

In the evening of the 7th of June, 1844, the guard at the prison were overpowered by a mob, who fired on Smith, his brother, and two of their fellow-prisoners. *Joseph Smith was shot dead while attempting to leap out of the window.* The murderers were never found out. It may be easily supposed that the unhappy end of this man excited the grief and indignation of even those who disbelieved his pretensions as a prophet. Among his followers it was looked on as a martyrdom.

Sidney Rigdon aspired to be the successor of Smith, and pretended to revelations which contradicted those of Smith. But he was expelled from the church for numerous offences, and the chief place was taken by Bingham Young. Under his guidance the temple was completed. They called Nauvoo "The Holy City." Their manner of expressing their joy in what they boasted to be a fulfilment of Smith's prophecy renewed the hostilities of their neighbours. They were again involved in war, which raged for months during the year after Smith's murder. Nauvoo was regularly besieged; and the Mormons were compelled to abandon it. They sought a home beyond the Rocky Mountains. They sent five hundred men to serve in the army of the United States in the war with Mexico. When the war ended, these disbanded soldiers settled in Upper California. Numbers of the exiles from Nauvoo went both by land and by sea to California, and were among the first of the gold-finders in that state. The greater part of them, however, proceeded by a long and terrible journey, which lasted many months, to the Great Salt Lake, east of California and south of the Oregon territory. This settlement is governed by Mr. Bingham Young, appointed by the president of the United States in 1850. To secure the amount of population required in order to enjoy the protection of the United States general government—which is sixty thousand, the apostles of the Mormons have gone to various parts of Europe that they might "gather the saints." It is stated in their reports that, at the beginning of the year 1851, there were upwards of thirty thousand "saints" in Great Britain and Ireland, and that about twenty thousand had emigrated from our shores to join the Mormons in America. In 1850, the number of emigrants from Liverpool was between two and three thousand. On their arrival at New Orleans, these emigrants go up the Mississippi by steam-boats to St. Louis, which is thirteen hundred miles; eight hundred miles further up they reach Council Bluffs, the half-way settlement on the overland journey to California. The rest of the journey, above a thousand miles, is performed in wagons drawn by oxen. The entire distance, by this route, from New Orleans to the Great Salt Lake City is more than three thousand miles, and the time spent in traversing this distance is three months. We are informed, however, that, in future, the emigrants will either cross the isthmus of Panama, or go by sea round Cape Horn.

There are contradictory reports of this new settlement with which it is not our present purpose to meddle. There are also conflicting accounts of the moral character of the "saints," on which we do not dwell in this place. We have said enough to show that Joseph Smith belongs to the class of *enthusiasts or deceivers*, whose appearance was foretold by the apostles of our Lord Jesus Christ.

1. We have *no proof* that he received messages from Heaven. Any man may *say* that he is inspired, and may get people to believe him; but neither his saying nor their believing proves it to be true. But Jesus and his apostles *proved* that they were messengers of God by their doctrine, their miracles, and their lives. The Mormonite witnesses say things which are opinions, or expressions of feeling, but not testimonies to the alleged *fact* of Smith's inspiration.

2. The account which Joseph Smith gave of his visions *contradicts the plain teaching of the New Testament*. There we are told that there must be "repentance towards God, and faith towards our Lord Jesus Christ," before there is forgiveness of sins; but Joseph Smith says that an angel told him that "his sins *were* forgiven." If an angel *had* told him so, the angel would have preached another gospel than that which was preached by the apostles of our Lord.

3. Smith's pretended vision about John the Baptist *contradicts the New Testament*. John the Baptist was sent "before" our Saviour to prepare the Jews for his coming. When Jesus was baptized by him, there came a voice from heaven, saying, "This is my beloved Son, in whom I am well pleased;" and John directed his disciples to Jesus as "the Lamb of God." John held no office in the church of the New Testament. He had left the world before that church was formed at Jerusalem. John could not confer "the priesthood of Aaron," for many reasons:—*first*, because that priesthood was confined to the sons of Aaron; *secondly*, because that priesthood was a shadow of the priesthood of Christ before he came to offer himself as "the Lamb of God:" *thirdly*, because an end was put to that priesthood by the sacrifice of Christ on the cross; *fourthly*, because there is only one Priest in the Christian church, in the proper sense of

that word, as one who stands between the worshippers and God as a Mediator; *fifthly*, because the New Testament teaches us that all true believers, *as* believers, are "a royal priesthood," "kings and priests unto God," "to offer up spiritual sacrifices, acceptable to God by Jesus Christ," 1 Peter ii. 5, 9; Rev. i. 5, 6; v. 9, 10. The men who represent themselves as ordained by John the Baptist—as acting under the directions of Peter, James, and John—and as holding the keys of the priesthood of Melchisedec, have jumbled together a number of names which show their ignorance, when making this representation, of the New Testament. The priesthood of Melchisedec differed from the priesthood of Aaron in this one particular especially—that, while Aaron's priesthood went from father to son, Melchisedec's was *confined to his own person*—not received from a father nor handed over to a son; and it is for this reason that the priesthood of our Lord was foretold as being—not "after the order of Aaron," but "after the order of Melchisedec." This is very fully shown in the seventh chapter of the Epistle to the Hebrews.

4. The account given of the *ordination* of Smith and Cowdrey *is inconsistent with itself*, as well as *with the New Testament*. They say that John the Baptist ordained them; though there is no proof that John was there, or that he had any commission to ordain them; and then, they say that they ordained one another. Neither the ordination from John, nor their ordination of one another to a priesthood which had been done away eighteen hundred years before in Christ, has any ground in the New Testament; and, as we have seen, they have no more right than other men have, that is, *no right at all*, to do anything in the name of Christ which is not warranted by the New Testament. There would be no end to the absurdities, blasphemies, follies, and crimes that might be perpetrated by weak or wicked men, if we were to listen to pretensions such as these.

5. The *revelations* which Joseph Smith pretended to receive from God were *for his own ease, comfort, power, or glory*. If Cowdrey was as really ordained as Smith, why did he not share the power; and why did he leave him? Is it not easy to see through the imposture of such revelations as the following? "It is wisdom in me that my servant Martin Harris should be an example unto the church, in laying his monies before the bishop of the church. And also

this is law unto every man that cometh unto his land to receive an inheritance, he shall do with his monies according as the law directs, and it is wisdom also that there should be lands purchased in Independence, for the place of the storehouse, and also for the house of printing." " Let all monies which can be spared, it mattereth not to me whether it be little or much, be sent up to the land of Zion, unto those I have appointed to receive it." " It is meet that my servant Joseph Smith junior should have a house built in which to live and translate." " If ye desire the mysteries of my kingdom, provide for him food and raiment, and whatsoever thing he needeth to accomplish the work wherewith I have commanded him; and if ye do it not, he shall remain unto them that have received him; in temporal labours thou shalt not have strength, for this is not thy calling." " And now I say unto you as pertaining to my boarding-house, which I commanded you to build for the boarding of strangers, let it be built unto my name, and let my name be named upon it, and let my servant Joseph and his house have place therein from generation to generation." Can any revelations more unlike those of the New Testament be conceived, or anything more worldly, selfish, cunning, and ambitious?

6. While there are all these proofs against Smith's pretensions, there are very *strong testimonies*, subscribed and sworn before magistrates in the United States, *to his gross immorality* of conduct, as a swearer, seducer, adulterer, robber, and murderer. We have examined some of those testimonies, and we have also examined some of the answers given to them by Mormonites. It is not easy always to reach the truth in such matters; but if the charges are unlikely, is it not more unlikely that such a man as his followers *acknowledge* Smith to have been, was a messenger of Jesus Christ? Yet we cannot shut our eyes to the evidences which have been given in America to the character of Smith, and his family. They are described by their neighbours, (and, when they quarrelled, by those whom they had deceived,) as visionaries, diggers for money, and of low moral character. The citizens of the American states do not persecute men for religious opinions; but they declared that Smith and his companions must be dealt with as traitors and criminals; and it was *not as a martyr for religion*, but as the victim of popular vengeance for real or

supposed crimes, that Joseph Smith lost his life. No excuse is here made for the murderers. But *their* criminality does not prove his innocence of the crimes laid to his charge; still less does it prove that he was not *a deceiver of the people in the pretences he made to Divine revelations.*

7. Whatever may be the *temporal advantages* now enjoyed by the Mormonites in their new territory, these have *nothing to do with the truth of Mormonism* as a religion. It is against this that we are here concerned to warn the reader. Error in religion is a worse thing than poverty. We look on the religious system of the Mormons as one which is built upon a falsehood. We are sure that the Bible is true. For the same reasons, we are sure that Mormonism is *not* true, and that *Joseph Smith was not a messenger inspired of God to teach mankind.* We do not believe the golden accounts given by his followers of the almost heavenly prosperity of their new city. All descriptions of this sort, given by men whose interest it is to encourage people to go to particular places, are found upon examination to be *greatly exaggerated.* But, even if they were all true, we are still to listen to the warning voice of our Lord, who commands us to take heed lest any man deceive us. The Mormonites do not tell you of the sufferings, and losses, and numberless miseries which must be undergone by men, women, and children, in travelling from England to the other side of the American continent; nor are we called on here to describe them. We confine our attention to one point, and that is—*the claims of Joseph Smith as a pretended prophet* of the Lord. We have shown the kind of proof there is for the belief which Christians hold in the Divine authority of the Bible. We have shown that the Bible foretells the appearance of deceivers. We have shown that many such deceivers have existed. We have shown at Joseph Smith has *no more right to be held as a prohet than Southcote, Brothers, Mohammed, Manes, Monnus, or Simon Magus.*—Having shown the contrast etween Christianity and Mormonism in their beginning and progress, we propose, in a second tract, to show the contrast of Christianity with Mormonism in their Books and Doctrines.

THE RELIGIOUS TRACT SOCIETY;
56, PATERNOSTER ROW, AND 65, ST. PAUL'S CHURCHYARD

[*Price* 6s. *per* 100]

A FEW PLAIN WORDS

ABOUT

MORMONISM,

SHOWING THAT

Latter-Day Saints are no Saints at all,

PROVED BY

𝕰𝖝𝖙𝖗𝖆𝖈𝖙𝖘 𝖋𝖗𝖔𝖒 𝖙𝖍𝖊𝖎𝖗 𝖂𝖗𝖎𝖙𝖎𝖓𝖌𝖘.

BY THE AUTHOR OF

A Few Plain Words about Popery & the Pope. 180th Thousand.
Pope or Queen, or What Should we do at the Coming Election.
&c. &c.

"But though we or an angel from heaven preach any other gospel unto you, than that which we have preached unto you, let him be accursed.—*Gal.* i. 8.

PRINTED AND PUBLISHED FOR THE AUTHOR,
BY JOHN WRIGHT, STEAM PRESS, BRISTOL.
LONDON: WERTHEIM & MACINTOSH, AND HOULSTON & STONEMAN,
PATERNOSTER ROW; AND
JAMES NISBET & Co. BERNERS STREET. OLIVER & BOYD, EDINBURGH.
Price Twopence each, or Twelve Shillings per Hundred.

A FEW PLAIN WORDS ABOUT MORMONISM.

Some few years ago I heard that a respectable young man in the country whose friends I knew very well, had joined the Mormonites or Latter Day Saints, and that in consequence he had sold off all his things, and taken his wife and children, mother and sister, to some place very far back in America, where all the sect were to live. I could not learn what they were to do there in particular, different from other people, except that a grand Temple was to be built, to which every one who joined them was expected to pay.

That people should emigrate to America is not so uncommon a thing as to occasion any surprise; the only oddity about it is, that any body should fancy that he *cannot* serve God here as well as anywhere else, since every person in this country is at liberty to worship God as he thinks right, so long as he does not harm his neighbours. It strikes me that *change of heart* is much more important in the matter of serving God, than *change of place*. The ancient Jews thought that acceptable worship could only be offered at *Jerusalem*, and their neighbours, the Samaritans, believed that *Mount Gerizim* was the place where men ought to worship; but our Lord taught them that, in the dispensation he was about to introduce, neither the one nor the other place was exclusively essential,—that God looks to the heart.

A year or two after this person had left the country, a letter came from him, in which he talked very large not only of what was going to happen to the nations of the earth, but of the part which he and his friends were going to take in it; no less than being horns of iron to push them together.

This young man was I believe a very decent person in his way—a country wheelwright, and doing a tidy business in the cart and wheelbarrow line, but assuredly none of his English friends imagined his abilities were of that stamp to be of much account in " pushing nations;" and if his new acquaintance led him to believe he was going to be so employed, they were much deceived; for not very long ago his friends heard that his body had been found dreadfully mutilated, supposed to have been robbed and murdered by the Indians.

Such was the melancholy end of his dreams of ruling over others; and as many thousand people have left this country with the same notions; and persons are now very busy in different parts of Great Britain trying to persuade others to take the same steps, I have been led to examine the principles and writings that teach we cannot be christians in *every country*, but must, if we would be saved, *forthwith* subscribe one tenth of our property to be laid out on building schemes in California, and prepare to break up our homes here, no matter how comfortably settled, or how unfit we may be for a change of country.

It is quite clear even to the simplest reader, that the *Bible* gives no warrant for all this, and therefore we are at once met with the assurance that the Bible is not enough for us, but that an Angel appeared to one Joseph Smith, and directed him to a certain stone box which had been hidden for 1400 years under ground, full of golden plates which were engraved with curious characters. We are told that he was directed to keep these plates from every body's sight; that in the box was an immense pair of spectacles, called Urim and Thummim, which he was to put on, and then he would be able to read the characters which an Angel would translate for him into English; and as he could not write himself, another person must copy it from his mouth.

Now I will not say that it is impossible for God to make a revelation of his will to Joseph Smith or anybody else. It does not belong to mortal man to say that God cannot do this or that thing; but we are quite safe in saying that if God should make another revelation to man, it will be one worthy of his character, as a Being of Infinite Holiness, Wisdom, and Love.

We are also quite safe in saying that any revelation from God intended for our use, would be such as to commend itself to our *understandings;* for God commands our obedience as a *reasonable* service. For instance we know the Bible to be the Word of God, because its contents agree with the *character* of God. It tells us what we could never have known, had not the wisdom of God revealed it to us in the Bible; and all the efforts of learned men in past ages to overthrow its authority, have only the more firmly established its truth.

We also observe that copies of the Scriptures in the ancient languages and of the greatest antiquity, are spread over the world. That these manuscripts are open to the inspection of the learned, that they have been examined and compared one with the other, both by enemies and friends. And of late years, by the discovery of the meaning of the figures on the Egyptian tombs in the pyramids, the truth of the Christian's Bible has been wonderfully confirmed; while, strange to relate, within the last twelve months, there has been dug up in the ruins of Nineveh, sculptured stones containing an account of the very sums paid by Hezekiah to the King of Nineveh.

We see then that the Bible not only declares itself to be the Word of God, but that it is *proved* to be so by every kind of testimony. Hence the most learned men who have investigated its claims acknowledge its authority, and even bad people whose practices it condemns, believe it is what it professes to be. Indeed so clear is the evidence of its divine authority, that it is impossible *after* a thorough *examination* of it, to be an unbeliever, for even those places which may appear at first sight to an unlearned person most difficult to explain, prove to be correct; and the researches of travellers and learned men in the present age, have made clear many things which puzzled our forefathers.

We may say of the Bible, like every other work of God, that the more it is examined, the more beautiful it appears; while the finest works of men when examined by a microscope, are full of defects and blemishes. Now I propose to apply this test to the Book of Mormon, which the Mormonites say is the Book of God too. If it be so, we shall certainly find the tokens of its divine author, for "as for God his work is perfect." We should not take a bank note without satisfying ourselves that it was genuine; how much less then should we receive that for a revelation of the Most High God, which we have not the most undoubted evidence is such.

If my master sends a letter to me with particular directions to do certain things, and a long time afterwards another letter contradicting it, is brought to me by a stranger who says he comes from my master, I should of course examine it very carefully, and if I find the writing not at all like what I *know* to be his, I naturally think it is not a true document, and pay no attention to it. Let us then in a spirit of fairness examine whether the Book of Mormon contains such marks as must stamp it in the mind of any plain person of ordinary common sense as an imposture, or whether it has such internal excellence as to be worthy of the origin claimed for it.

The Book of Mormon is a volume containing about two thirds as much as the Old Testament. It consists of fourteen separate books, said to have been written at different times by different persons, extending over a period of about 1000 years, from about 600 years before Christ to the year of our Lord 420, when the plates from which Smith's translation is said to be made, were hid in a stone box in a hill called Cumorah, in the State of New York, by the prophet Moroni. The purport of the book is to teach that America is the Land of Promise, that Mount Zion is there, and that all who do not flee there will perish.

It principally relates in very clumsy and ungrammatical language the wars and contentions of nations who are said to have once lived on the American continent, and of one family of whom the present American Indians are said to be the descendants. We are informed that America was first peopled at the time of the building of the *Tower of Babel* by a party of 22 persons; these became mighty nations who were totally destroyed from off the land just before the arrival of a small party of Jews from Jerusalem, in the first year of Zedekiah king of Judah. They had left their sacred records on gold plates which fell into the hands of the new comers. This party it seems crossed the Pacific Ocean, and landed on the Western coast of South America. Ten years afterwards another party left Jerusalem, who landed in North America; and with the adventures of this last colony the Book of Mormon commences. It states that a pious Jew named Lehi, who lived in Jerusalem in the time of Zedekiah, was commanded by God to take his family and depart into the wilderness.

"And it came to pass that the Lord commanded my father, even in a dream, that he should take his family and depart into the wilderness. And it came to pass that he was obedient unto the word of the Lord, wherefore he did as the Lord commanded him.

And it came to pass that he departed into the wilderness. And he left his house, and the land of his inheritance, and his gold and his silver, and his precious things, and took nothing with him save it were his family, and provisions, and tents, and departed into the wilderness; and he came down by the borders near the shore of the Red Sea; and he travelled in the wilderness in the borders which are near the Red Sea; and he did travel in the wilderness with his family, which consisted of my mother Sariah, and my elder brothers, who were Laman, Lemuel, and Sam.

And it came to pass that when he had travelled three days in the wilderness, he pitched his tent in a valley by the side of a river of water. And it came to pass that he built an altar of stones, and made an offering unto the Lord, and gave thanks unto the Lord our God." *Page* 3.

After a time Lehi had a dream, in which he was commanded to send his sons back to Jerusalem, to get some plates of brass which contained the Law and the genealogy of their families, which were in the hands of one Laban, of the same tribe, who would not give them up, and drove them away; but Nephi came back in the night, and gives this account of his proceedings:

"And I was led by the Spirit, not knowing beforehand the things which I should do. Nevertheless I went forth, and as I came near unto the house of Laban, I beheld a man, and he had fallen to the earth before me, for he was drunken with wine. And when I came to him I found that it was Laban. And I beheld his sword, and I drew it forth from the sheath thereof, and the hilt thereof was of pure gold, and the workmanship thereof was exceeding fine: and I saw that the blade thereof was of the most precious steel.

And it came to pass that I was constrained by the Spirit that I should kill Laban; but I said in my heart, never at any time have I shed the blood of man; and I shrunk and would that I might not slay him. And the Spirit said unto me again, behold the Lord hath delivered him into thy hands; yea, and I also knew that he had sought to take away mine own life; yea, and he would not hearken unto the commandments of the Lord; and he also had taken away our property.

And it came to pass that the Spirit said unto me again, slay him, for the Lord hath delivered him into thy hands. Behold the Lord slayeth the wicked to bring forth his righteous purposes. It is better that one man should perish, than that a nation should dwindle and perish in unbelief.

And now, when I, Nephi, had heard these words, I remembered the words of the Lord which he spake unto me in the wilderness, saying, that inasmuch as thy seed shall keep my commandments, they shall prosper in the *land of promise*. Yea, and I also thought that they could not keep the commandments of the Lord according to the law of Moses, save they should have the law. And I also knew that the law was engraven upon the plates of brass. And again—I knew that the Lord had delivered Laban into my hands for this cause, that I might obtain the records according to his commandments. Therefore I did obey the voice of the Spirit, and took Laban by the hair of the head, and I smote off his head with his own sword." *Page* 8.

Here we see the Holy Spirit of God is made to use the very argument which the Apostle says is damnable, "to do evil that good may come," and to incite to wilful murder and robbery; for from what follows, it does not appear but what these pretended plates really belonged to Laban. But let us proceed. Nephi and his brothers returned with the plates to their father:

"And it came to pass that they did rejoice exceedingly, and did offer sacrifices and burnt offerings unto the Lord; and they gave thanks unto the God of Israel. * * And it came to pass that my father Lehi also found upon the plates of brass, a genealogy of his fathers; WHEREFORE he knew that he was a descendant of Joseph. * * And *thus* my father Lehi did discover the genealogy of his fathers. And Laban also was a descendant of Joseph, *wherefore* he and his fathers had kept the records." *Page* 11.

Now I do not hesitate to affirm, that the above Extracts, brief as they are, and extending only to the eleventh page of the book, contain so much of absurdity and contradiction, as will upon examination convince the simplest believer in the Bible, that he must give up either the Book of Mormon, or the Book of God, for that they cannot both be true. Let us examine these statements, and compare them with the Bible.

First. That a Jew and his family are commanded to leave Judea, to be taken to a *Land of Promise*, which turns out to be America.

Now this is flatly contradicted by God's express words, for his promise to Abram was,

"Unto thy seed have I given *this* land, from the river of Egypt unto the great river, the river Euphrates." *Gen.* xv. 18.

Second. That a family of pious Jews rejoiced and offered sacrifices and burnt offerings in the *wilderness*, being descendants of *Joseph*.

Here are *two* palpable contradictions to God's Word.

1. They are said to offer sacrifices *in the wilderness*, but God's express law was on this wise:

"But *when* ye go over Jordan, and dwell in the land which the Lord your God giveth you to inherit, and *when* he giveth you rest from all your enemies round about, so that ye dwell in safety; then there shall be a *place* which the Lord your God shall *choose* to cause his name to dwell there; *thither* shall ye bring all that I command you; your burnt offerings, and your sacrifices, your tithes, and the heave offering of your hand, and all your choice vows which ye vow unto the Lord. And ye shall rejoice before the Lord your God, ye, and your sons, and your daughters, and your menservants, and your maidservants, and the Levite that is within your gates; forasmuch as he hath no part nor inheritance with you. *Take heed* to thyself that thou *offer not* thy burnt offerings in *every place* that thou seest: but in the place which the Lord shall choose in one of thy tribes, *there* thou shalt offer thy burnt offerings, and there thou shalt do all that I command thee." *Deut.* xii. 10, 14.

2. The descendants of *Joseph* had no right to offer sacrifices and burnt offerings unto the Lord, for it was strictly prohibited in the Law, and for this very crime Korah and his company were destroyed. God set apart the descendants of *Aaron* to offer sacrifice, and expressly forbade every other, under pain of death.

And Eleazar the priest took the brazen censers wherewith they that were burnt had offered; and they were made broad plates for a covering of the altar, to be a memorial unto the children of Israel, that *no stranger* which is not of the seed of *Aaron*, come near to offer incense before the Lord, that he be not as Korah and his company." *Numbers* xvi. 39, 40.

"Therefore thou and thy sons with thee, [Aaron] shall keep your priests' office for every thing of the altar, and within the vail, and ye shall serve: I have given your priests' office as a service of gift; *and the stranger that cometh nigh shall be put to death.*" *Numbers* xviii. 7.

We have now to notice the ridiculous absurdity that Lehi did not know "the genealogy of his fathers" till he had these plates from Laban. That is, he actually did not know what tribe he was of, although he was a married man with a grown up family. Now to fully understand the nonsense of this, we must bear in mind that every head of a family, except of the tribe of Levi, had an estate given to him by Joshua, which land could not be sold. If there had been nothing else therefore to tell him, the very possession of this estate was public proof, as plain as the sun at noon day, of the tribe to which he belonged; besides which we know there was nothing about which a Jew was more particular than his genealogy, which was kept in public registers, down to the time of Christ. If Lehi and his children did not know they were descendants of Joseph, we must also assume that when he married, his wife's family did not know the tribe of their new relative, and that in their intercourse with other Jews, they had never heard of it. Why it is just as impossible as for a man who is walking every day to be ignorant that he has the use of his legs.

After sojourning some years in the wilderness, Nephi the son of Lehi, was filled with wisdom to build a ship, the "workmanship whereof was exceeding fine," in which they all embarked for America; but after some days it is said, the brothers of Nephi were "lifted up into exceeding rudeness," and bound him with cords. "And it came "to pass that after they had bound me, insomuch that I could not move, "the compass which had been prepared of the Lord, did cease to work, "wherefore they knew not whither they should steer the ship." After some days however they loosed Nephi, and then we are told, "And it "came to pass after they had loosed me, behold I *took the compass*, and it "did work *whither I desired it.*" *Page* 43.

Now all this must certainly be Joseph Smith's, and no angel's, for it is pure nonsense. Smith was an ignorant countryman, born and bred some hundreds of miles from the sea side; he had *heard* of a compass, but most certainly had never *seen* one, and had not the least idea of the way in which it is used, or he could never have talked about "*taking it*," and its "*working whither he desired.*"

It cannot surely be necessary to quote more evidence in proof of its being not only an imposture, but one that can only delude the most ignorant of mankind. But it may be well in another interesting particular, to compare it with God's own blessed Word. The books of the Bible were written at different periods widely apart. It is known that some Books were written during and after the Babylonish Captivity; and accordingly, as might be expected, there is a gradual change in the language, from the pure Hebrew of the earlier parts, to the mixed Hebrew and Chaldaic. Now in the Book of Mormon we have continually a style of writing belonging to a later age, used before its time. We have words pretended to be written at a time in which they were not in use, and the same word being used in different languages at the same time. All these blunders are impossible to divine inspiration, but marvellously like the imposture of an ignorant man who did not know the meaning of the words he was using.

For instance, the words *Messiah* and *Christ* are the same, the one being Hebrew and the other Greek, both meaning the "anointed." Hebrew writers therefore who lived hundreds of years before the Greek language was used, could not use Greek expressions; and we never find the word Christ in the *Old* Testament, but *Messiah;* but it is used repeatedly in the Book of Mormon, for Nephi the Jew, who lived 600 years before Christ, continually uses this Greek word:

"For according to the words of the prophets, the Messiah cometh in six hundred years from the time that my father left Jerusalem, and according to the words of the prophets, and also the word of the Angel of God, his name shall be Jesus Christ, the Son of God." *Page* 97.

The same may be said of the terms "Holy Ghost," and "Bible;" both are words that could not have been used by an ancient Jew who wrote at the time the Book of Mormon is said to have been written. The word "Bible" is of very late date. The Jews had no word to express its meaning, for "*they had no Bible.*" Their sacred writings were termed the Law, the Prophets, and the Writings. But Joseph Smith makes Nephi prophesy of us who will not believe his revelations, as follows:

"And my words shall hiss forth unto the ends of the earth, for a standard unto my people, which are of the house of Israel. And because my words shall hiss forth, many of the Gentiles shall say, a bible, a bible, we have got a bible, and there cannot be any more bible." "Thou fool, that shalt say, a bible, we have got a bible, and we need no more Bible." "And because that I have spoken one word, ye need not suppose that I cannot speak another; for my work is not yet finished; neither shall it be, until the end of man; neither from that time henceforth and for ever. Wherefore, because that ye have a bible, ye need not suppose that it contains all my words; neither need ye suppose that I have not caused more to be written." *Page* 107.

I might multiply these passages by hundreds, in which the words Jesus Christ, Holy Ghost, Bible, Alpha and Omega, and other phrases, prove indisputably that the whole book is a *modern* imposture. What would be thought if I pretended to have found an old Monkish Journal a thousand years old, in which the writer should give an account of his journey to some Saint's tomb in Scotland, in language like this.

"I took the omnibus which passes the door of our Monastery, to the 'Bristol Station, and left by the express train. At Swindon I got a cup 'of tea and a sandwich. On my arrival at Paddington, I discovered I 'had left behind, my umbrella and portmanteau; but they were tele-'graphed for, and in the evening a policeman brought them to me in the 'coffee room. I felt too tired to walk, and therefore took a cab to the 'Edinburgh Steam Packet Office. I made the man drive a little out 'of his way that I might see the Crystal Palace, in which the Great 'Exhibition was held, of which I read so much in the newspapers. I 'noticed in passing, the new Parliament Houses, and the statues of the 'Duke of Wellington at Hyde Park and the Exchange, but above all, the 'splendour of the plate glass in the shops, and the brilliancy of the gas in 'the streets."

What would be thought of the person who pretended that this was a translation from an ancient document? and yet the Book of Mormon is just as barefaced an imposture as this would be. I shall refer to but one more of the books, which though placed last in the volume, is the first in point of time. The book of Ether professes to give an account of an emigration to America, at the time of the building of Babel; and a very remarkable voyage it must have been,—shut up with 'flocks and herds," in close vessels, without any air to breathe, but what they got by unplugging a hole, for upwards of *Eleven Months.*

"And it came to pass that the brother of Jared did go to work, and also his brethren, and built barges after the manner which they had built, according to the instructions of the Lord. And they were small, and they were light upon the water, even like unto the lightness of a fowl upon the water; and they were built after a manner that they were exceeding tight, even that they would hold water like unto a dish; and the bottom thereof was tight like unto a dish; and the sides thereof were tight like unto a dish; and the ends thereof were peaked; and the top thereof was tight like unto a dish; and the length thereof was the length of a tree; and the door thereof, when it was shut, was tight like unto a dish. And it came to pass that the brother of Jared cried unto the Lord, saying, O Lord I have performed the work which thou hast commanded me, and I have made the barges according as thou hast directed me. And behold, O Lord, in them there is no light, whither shall we steer. And also we shall perish, for in them we cannot breathe, save it is the air which is in them; therefore we shall perish. And the Lord said unto the brother of Jared, behold, thou shalt make a hole in the top thereof, and also in the bottom thereof; and when thou shalt suffer for air, thou shalt unstop the hole thereof, and receive air. And if it be so that the water come in upon thee, behold, ye shall stop the hole thereof, that ye may not perish in the flood." *Page* 520.

"And it came to pass that when they had prepared all manner of food, that thereby they might subsist upon the water, and also food for their flocks and herds, and whatsoever beast, or animal, or fowl that they could carry with them. And it came to pass that when they had done all these things, they got aboard of their vessels or barges, and set forth into the sea, commending themselves unto the Lord their God. And it came to pass that the Lord God caused that there should a furious wind blow upon the face of the waters, towards the promised land; and thus they were tossed upon the waves of the sea before the wind. And it came to pass that they were many times buried in the depths of the sea, because of the mountain waves which broke upon them, and also the great and terrible tempests which were caused by the fierceness of the wind. * * And thus they were driven forth, three hundred and forty and four days upon the water; and they did land upon the shore of the promised land." *Page* 527.

It seems they attained to great prosperity, but got quarrelsome, and their warfare must have been of a curious sort, for they could *lay siege to a wilderness!*

"And it came to pass that the brother of Shared did give battle unto him in the wilderness of Akish: and the battle became exceeding sore, and many thousands fell by the sword. And it came to pass that Coriantumr *did lay siege to the wilderness*, and the brother of Shared did march forth out of the wilderness by night, and slew a part of the army of Coriantumr, as they were drunken." *Page* 545.

At length one universal desire for slaughter seems to have possessed the whole nation, for we are told:

"And it came to pass that when they were all gathered together, every one to the army which he would, with their wives and their children; both men, *women*, and *children being armed* with weapons of war, having shields, and breast-plates, and head-plates, and being clothed after the manner of war, they did march forth one against another, to battle." *Page* 548.

The conclusion of this bloody tragedy forcibly reminds one of the Irishman's cats in a sawpit, which ate each other up all but the tail.

"And it came to pass that when they had all fallen by the sword, save it were Coriantumr and Shiz, behold Shiz had fainted with loss of blood. And it came to pass that when Coriantumr had leaned upon his sword, that he rested a little, he smote off the head of Shiz. And it came to pass that AFTER he had smote off the head of Shiz, that Shiz *raised upon his hands* and fell; and after he had struggled for breath, he died. And it came to pass that Coriantumr fell to the earth, and became as if he had no life." *Page* 549.

This Shiz must have been an extraordinary fellow, and it is a pity that he did not in return cut off Coriantumr's head; the narrative would then have been complete. Such however in sober seriousness, is a fair sample of the book which is alleged to have been dictated by the Holy Spirit of God, and to be of equal authority with the Old and New Testaments.

To have gone through the whole book, would have made this tract as large as the Bible itself: besides, we may tell the flavour of a leg of mutton from a *slice*, as well as if we ate the whole joint. I do not take much notice of the *incorrect language*, though it is not unfair to argue that if an Angel were sent from heaven to translate modern Egyptian into English, he would use *good* English, whereas the *whole* of the Book of Mormon is full of grammatical blunders, *except in the chapters taken from our Bible;* and this is a very curious fact, that though (as we are told) the angel inspired Joseph Smith with the *whole* translation, that part of it which contains matter similar to our Bible is correct, while all the rest is manifestly the writing of an ignorant man. The Mormonites allow that Smith was unlettered, and affirm that the whole book was taken down from angel's lips. How comes it then that the *new* matter is full of such blunders as an uneducated man would certainly make, while the *old* is quite correct. They would have us to believe that an Angel translates whole chapters of Isaiah from Egyptian, in precisely the same words as our translators used, and in other places makes blunders for which a common school boy would be whipped. Why this, if true, would be a miracle equal to that of finding the box itself.

The Mormonites say that this incorrectness is intended by the Spirit of God as a trial of the faith of the simple hearted; but if we allow that an angel might write very bad English, it must be granted that none but an angel of darkness could be concerned in stating absurdities and positive untruths, which plainly contradict the Word of God.

If the whole of the writings and teachings of Mormonism were confined to the Book of Mormon, we might safely let it alone, for it is such absurd, and (at the same time) such stupid stuff, that I am sure but few even of themselves read it. But Joseph Smith had an end in view, beside urging people to come to America;—they must not only come to America, but to that place in it which would suit his purpose, and when there, they must be governed by himself and his colleagues. He had found a dupe in a credulous farmer named Martin Harris, who advanced money to print his book, and picked up Sidney Rigdon and Oliver Cowdery, two associates who had more learning than himself and as little principle. It is an old saying, that one lie needs more support it, and Smith soon found that the revelation of the Book of Mormon needed others to back it. These have been collected together and published under the title of "The Book of Doctrines and Covenants," which contains as much of absurdity and contradiction, as the "Book of Mormon" itself, while the following which is only one among many, shows that Smith knew how to take care of himself and his associates:

"And again, it is mete that my servant Joseph Smith, jun., should have a house built in which to live and translate. And again, it is mete that my servant Sidney Rigdon should live as seemeth him good, inasmuch as he keepeth my commandments." *Doctrines and Covenants, Page* 214. *February,* 1831.

Again, whenever Joseph had a question put to him which he found it inconvenient to answer, he had a revelation forthwith, forbidding him to reply to it. For instance, Martin Harris got a little suspicious about the Plates, and very naturally wished to *see* them; Joseph forthwith had the following revelation, which you will observe, while it rebukes Harris, and establishes Joseph's supreme authority, holds out a hope that he shall see the Plates some time, if he is humble enough.

"Behold, I say unto you, that as my servant Martin Harris has desired a witness at my hand, that you, my servant Joseph Smith, jun., have got the plates of which you have testified and borne record that you have received of me; and now, behold, this shall you say unto him, he who spake unto you said unto you, I, the Lord, am God, and have given these things unto you, my servant Joseph Smith, Jun., and have commanded you that you should stand as a witness of these things, and I have caused you that you should enter into a covenant with me, that you *should not show them except to those persons to whom I commanded you*; and you have no power over them except I grant it unto you. * * Behold, if they will not believe my words, they would not believe you, my servant Joseph, if it were possible that you could show them all these things which I have committed unto you. Oh! this unbelieving and stiffnecked generation, mine anger is kindled against them.

Behold, verily I say unto you, I have reserved those things which I have entrusted unto you, my servant Joseph, for a wise purpose in me, and it shall be made known unto future generations; but this generation shall have my word *through you;* and in addition to your testimony, the testimony of three of my servants, whom I shall call and ordain, unto whom I will show these things, and they shall go forth with my words that are given through you.

And now, again, I speak unto you, my servant Joseph, concerning the man that desires the witness. Behold, I say unto him, he exalts himself and does not humble himself sufficiently before me; but if he will bow down before me, and humble himself in mighty prayer and faith, in the sincerity of his heart, then will I grant unto him a view of the things which he desires to see." *Doctrines and Covenants, March,* 1829. *Page* 171.

This quieted Harris for a time, but it would seem that he again got uneasy, and needed other revelations to keep him up to the mark, in one of which he is commanded not to "*covet* his own property."

Wherefore I command you to repent, and keep the commandments which you have received by the hand of my servant, Joseph Smith, jun., in my name. * * And again I command thee that thou shalt not covet thine own property, but impart it freely to the printing of the Book of Mormon, which contains the truth and the word of God.

Behold, this is a great and the last commandment which I shall give unto you concerning this matter; for this shall suffice for thy daily walk, even unto the end of thy life. And misery thou shalt receive if thou wilt slight these counsels; yea, even the destruction of thyself and property. Impart a portion of thy property; yea, even part of thy lands, and all save the support of thy family. Pay the debt thou hast contracted with the printer." *Doctrines and Covenants, Page* 194. *March,* 1830.

"And now I give unto you further directions concerning this land. It is wisdom in me that my servant Martin Harris should be an example unto the church, in *laying his monies* before the bishop of the church. *Doctrines and Covenants, Page* 144.

When Harris had sufficiently "humbled himself," the following wonderful testimony was published, signed by Martin Harris, Oliver Cowdery, and David Whitmer, and upon this *very curious* evidence, the whole world is required to swallow Joseph Smith's narrative.

"And they have been shown unto us by the *power of God*, and not of man; and we declare, with words of soberness, that an Angel of God came down from heaven; and he brought and laid before our eyes, that we beheld and saw the plates."

Of all the rhodomontade ever pretended to be given as evidence of the truth of any fact, perhaps this is about the worst. If we wanted proof that the whole thing was Smith's own fabrication, we surely have it here in this pretended testimony. Smith says he had certain plates in his possession which none else must see till he had permission to show them. Suppose we take him at his word, what could be more simple and easy, when he had this permission, than for him to let these people look at them. If a man wants to convince me that he has a guinea in his pocket, the shortest way is for him to pull it out, and that satisfies me at once. What need for an angel to come from heaven to do that which Smith himself could have done as effectually in one minute.

The value of the evidence is not strengthened either when we examine the characters of the witnesses. Harris, we have seen, was the poor dupe whose only chance of getting back his money depended on the sale of the book. Oliver Cowdery may be better estimated by a revelation which Smith found it necessary to have concerning him on this wise:

"It is not wisdom in me that Oliver Cowdery should be entrusted with the commandments and *the monies* which he shall carry into the land of Zion, *except one go with* him who will be *true* and *faithful*." *Doctrines and Covenants, November,* 1831.

And we afterwards find his name, with that of David Whitmer, in a document drawn up by Rigdon, (and signed by eighty-four of their own people,) wherein they are declared to be "united with a gang of counterfeiters, thieves, liars, and blacklegs of the deepest die, to deceive, cheat, and defraud the saints out of their property." So that we see the lying absurdity of the testimony matches wonderfully well with the characters of those who put it forth.

I have hitherto confined my observations to the two books which, though perhaps little read, are the standards of the Mormonist's faith, and were published in the lifetime of the founder of the sect. It sometimes however happens that the practical working of a system may be better than we should suppose from its origin, and that when it gets adopted by fresh parties, much that was objectionable in its origin becomes, as it were, out of use and forgotten. I have therefore examined some of the later Mormonite works, published by their greatest living writer, Orson Pratt.

"For seventeen hundred years the nations upon the eastern hemisphere have been entirely destitute of the " *kingdom of God.*" "The King occasionally visited his subjects in ancient times, and once tarried with them for several years: but he received such cruel abuse from many of the people, that he left them, and went to some other part of his dominions. Where the King is gone the people cannot tell. I will now tell you the reason why the King has kept silence so long. It is because he has had no subjects to converse with; all have turned away from him, and advocated other governments as being the rightful and legal authority. They killed off and utterly destroyed every true subject of his kingdom, and *left not a vestige upon earth.*" *The Kingdom of God, Pages* 1, 2, 3.

Who of us has not heard or read of the martyrs who have died for the testimony of Jesus, rejoicing in the flames that they were counted worthy to suffer for his sake? who of us has not known some friend, or perhaps relative, who has departed in the faith, rejoicing in the hope that maketh not ashamed, and bearing joyful testimony that the Saviour's presence lighted their passage through the dark valley? Yet according to this Mormon writer, all this is a delusion, and we are to believe that the whole world has been destitute of the Kingdom of God, till the appearance of Joseph Smith, every stage of whose career is marked with imposture and ignorance.

With respect to the following quotations I will say but little, the subject is too awful; read them attentively, and with earnest prayer to God that his Holy Spirit may ever preserve you from such dreadful delusions. The path of error is a downward road, and the miserable victims who venture on it, do not know to what depths they may fall. It is the blessed privilege of the humblest christian to know that his Father is ever near, to hear and to answer his feeblest cry, and that when even two or three may be gathered together to seek him, he is in the midst of them; but of the wretched Mormons and the monster of their own creation whom they term God, may it not be said as of the priests of Baal, when they cried aloud to him, "But there was no voice, nor any that answered." And might we not say as Elijah did, "Cry aloud, for your God; either he is talking, or he is pursuing, or he is on a journey, or peradventure he sleepeth, and must be awaked?" How can a Mormonite pray when he believes that the deity he worships cannot be in two places at once? I dare not dwell on this; but I entreat you prayerfully to compare the passages of God's word with the Mormonite doctrines opposite, and you will not need other proof to convince you that Mormonism and Christianity are as opposed to each other as light is to darkness.

"The whole person of the FATHER consists of innumerable parts; and each part is so situated as to bear certain relations of distance to every other part. There must also be to a certain degree, a freedom of motion among these parts, which is an *essential condition to the movement of* HIS LIMBS without which he could only move as a whole."

"The Holy Spirit being one part of the Godhead, is also a MATERIAL SUBSTANCE of the same nature and properties in many respects, as the spirits of the Father and Son. It exists in vast immeasurable quantities in connexion with all material worlds. God the Father and God the Son cannot be everywhere present; indeed they *cannot be even in two places at the same instant;* but God the Holy Spirit is omnipresent—it extends through all space, intermingling with all other matter, yet no one *atom of the Holy Spirit can be in two places at the same instant,* which in all cases is an absolute impossibility. Each *atom of* the Holy Spirit is intelligent, and like all other matter has *solidity, form,* and *size,* and *occupies space.* Two atoms of this spirit cannot occupy the same space at the same time, neither can one atom, as before stated, occupy two separate spaces at the same time. *In all these respects it does not differ in the least from all other matter.* * * Two persons receiving the gift of the Holy Spirit, do not each receive at the same time the same identical particles, though they each receive a substance exactly similar in kind. It would be as impossible for each to receive the same identical atoms at the same instant, as it would be for two men at the same time to drink the same identical pint of water."

"As the persons of the Father and Son cannot be everywhere present, it is therefore impossible for them to attend in *person* to all the multiplied affairs of government among intelligent beings. *Ibid. Page* 5.

MORMONISM.

"The true God exists both in time and in space, and has as much relation to them as man or any other being. He has extension, and form, and dimensions, as well as man. He occupies space; has a body, parts, and passions; can go from place to place, can eat, drink, and talk, as well as man. Man resembles him in the features and form of his body, and he does not differ materially in size.

"The Godhead consists of the Father, the Son, and the Holy Spirit. The FATHER is a material being. The *substance* of which he is composed is *wholly material.* It is a substance widely different in some respects from the various substances with with which we are more immediately acquainted. In other respects it is precisely like all other materials. The substance of *his person* occupies space the same as other matter. It has *solidity, length, breadth,* and *thickness,* like all other matter. The elementary materials of his body are not susceptible of occupying, at the same time, the same identical space with other matter. The substance of his person, like other matter, *cannot be in two places at the same instant.* It also requires *time* for him to transport himself from place to place." *The Kingdom of God, Page* 4.

BIBLE.

"Will I eat the flesh of bulls, or drink the blood of goats."—*Psalm* l. 3.

"*Am* I a God at hand, saith the Lord, and not a God afar off? Can any hide himself in secret places that I shall not see him? saith the Lord. Do not I fill heaven and earth? saith the Lord." *Jer.* xxiii. 23, 24.

"Whither shall I go from thy spirit? or whither shall I flee from thy presence? If I ascend up into heaven, thou *art* there: if I make my bed in hell, behold, thou *art there.* If I take the wings of the morning, and dwell in the uttermost parts of the sea; Even there shall thy hand lead me, and thy right hand shall hold me." *Psalm* cxxxix. 7, 10.

"No man hath seen God at any time; the only begotten Son, which is in the bosom of the Father, he hath declared him." *John* i. 18.

"And he said, Thou canst not see my face; for there shall no man see me, and live." *Exodus* xxxiii. 20.

We know from the Bible, that there is but One Mediator between God and men, the man Christ Jesus, who ever liveth to make intercession for us; but Mormonism dethrones Jesus Christ, and puts Joseph Smith in his place. In their 281st hymn they say of Smith,

Of noble seed, of *heavenly birth,*
He came to bless the sons of earth;
O'er the world that was wrapt in silent night,
Like the sun, he spread his golden light.

The Saints, the Saints, his only pride,
For them he lived, for them he died!
Unchanged in death, with a Saviour's love,
He pleads their cause in the courts above.

I have hitherto examined only the RELIGIOUS pretensions of Mormonism, but it has another bait to cover its poisoned hook; and I fear that many who would have laughed at Smith's lying revelations, have been ensnared by the promises of riches and happiness in a distant Mormon settlement. But when we look closer at their emigration scheme, we shall see that it has produced, and can produce, nothing but misery and ruin; and that this alone furnishes proof positive, that the whole system is based on delusion.

Smith's first revelation announced that heaven upon earth was to be established at Kirtland in Pennsylvania; but when his bank there broke, and made it necessary for him to decamp, another pretended revelation fixed it in Missouri:

"Hearken, O ye elders of my church, *saith the Lord your God*, who have assembled yourselves together, according to my commandments, in this land, which is the *land of Missouri*, which is the land which I *have appointed and consecrated* for the gathering of the Saints: wherefore this is the land of promise, and the place for the *city of Zion*. And thus saith the Lord your God, if you will receive wisdom, here is wisdom. Behold, the place which is now called Independence, is the centre place, and a spot for the temple is lying westward, upon a lot which is not far from the court house: wherefore it is wisdom that the land should be purchased by the Saints; and also every tract lying westward, even unto the line running directly between Jew and Gentile. And also every tract bordering by the prairies, inasmuch as my disciples are enabled to buy lands. Behold, this is wisdom, that they may obtain it for an *everlasting inheritance*." *Doctrines and Covenants, Page* 165. *July* 1831.

Nothing could be more positive than this, and accordingly his dupes spent their substance in building a splendid temple at Nauvoo; but their domineering spirit and scandalous immoralities, aroused the bad feelings of the people about them; bloody quarrels arose, the end of which was the murder of Smith and his brother, and the forcible expulsion of the whole body out of the State. Their famed Temple was burnt, and not one stone remains upon another in the spot which they were made to believe was appointed by God himself to be the place of gathering for all the Saints upon earth.

The poor dupes were now told that Zion was in the mountains of California, and their road to it for thousands of miles across the Rocky Mountains might be tracked by the graves of the miserable victims who perished in the way. No sooner however had they become settled a little, than the bitter fruits of Mormonism which had caused their expulsion from Missouri began to appear in their new city, and officers were appointed by the United States government, to visit the Salt Lake city, and report on the state of society there. Let us read what they say.

"We deem it our duty to state in this official communication, that polygamy, or plurality of wives is openly avowed and practised in the territory under the sanction of, and in obedience to, the direct commands of the Church. So universal is this practice, that very few, if any, leading men in that community, can be found who have not more than one wife each. The prominent men in the church, whose example in all things it is the ambition of the more humble to imitate, have each many wives; some of them we are credibly informed and believe, as many as 20 or 30, and Brigham Young, the Governor, even a greater number. Only a few days before we left the territory, the Governor was seen riding through the streets of the city in an omnibus, with a large company of his wives, more than two thirds of whom had infants in their arms. It is not uncommon to find two or more sisters married to the same man; and in one instance at least, a mother and her two daughters, are among the wives of a leading member of the church." *Times, January* 20.

Reader, if you have ever listened to the glowing descriptions of a Mormonite preacher, when he was describing the happiness of those who went to this paradise in California, did he tell you that these *omnibus rides* formed any part of the enjoyments of the Saints? And is this the sort of heaven upon earth to which you would like to take a daughter, or a sister, or a wife? Do you think a state of society such as this, is likely to be one of peace, or of strife and contention? By the laws of the United States, when the population of any region before unoccupied, amounts to a certain number, they may claim of Congress to be made a Separate and Independent State of the Union; and the Mormon leaders in pitching upon California for their new Zion, though they had found a fertile home, far out of the way of other people, where they could establish a Government of their own, with a Mormon Governor, and Mormon Judges and Officers of every class. Here then was a prospect open to them, enough to tempt and satisfy the loftiest ambition; and their own Hymn Book (Hymn 290th) lets out that the secret of their anxiety to get their converts to California, is to aid in such projects as these:

We'll burst off all our fetters and break the Gentile yoke;
For long it has beset us, but now it shall be broke;
No more shall Jacob bow his neck;

Henceforth he shall be great and free,
In Upper California. O that's the land for me.
We'll reign, we'll rule, and triumph, and God shall be our king,
The plains, the hills, and vallies, shall with hosannas ring.

Every Mormonite preacher is in fact a recruiting sergeant for Brigham Young and his associates. Already there are tokens of war and bloodshed, which give us every reason to believe that the attempted reign of the Saints will end in their being put down as rebels against the general government of the United States, for the latest intelligence is this:

"The Mormons in the Utah territory are alleged to contemplate some act of defiance against the authority of the Federal Government, and as they are regarded with an animosity as unscrupulous as their own fanaticism, there will probably be a new assault upon them, which will end only with their extermination. It is said they were already arming and fortifying themselves, and had published a declaration of independence. As thousands of the working classes of England are understood to be preparing to join these people during the ensuing summer, a knowledge of the state of affairs may possibly check their infatuation." *Times, March* 18.

I give no opinion about Emigration in general, it may or may not be best in your particular case, but I trust I have satisfied you from their *own writings*, that the *religious* principles of Mormonism are entirely opposed to the Word of God; and let your own common sense decide whether a journey of 10,000 miles, to engage in a rebellion against the United States, can be the way to comfort and prosperity in this world, or to happiness in the world to come.

John Wright, Steam Press, Thomas Street, Bristol.

CHRISTIAN DEMOCRACY

A Church for our Day

BY
JULIE JEPHSON

LONDON
T. FISHER UNWIN
PATERNOSTER SQUARE
1902

[All rights reserved.]

CHRISTIAN DEMOCRACY

A Church for our Day

In these days of religious controversy and ecclesiastical conflict it may interest many to hear something of the most democratic and undoctrinal of all Christian Churches—the Independent or Congregational Church.

It is curious how much ignorance prevails amongst all classes as to the position of the Congregational Church, even though Dr. Fairbairn's works are widely known. That he is but one, though foremost, of a band of theological scholars and Christian workers who are slowly but surely gaining way, does not appear to be realised; it is not realised even by those who are on the watch-towers of thought.

Nearly every word written by the Dean of Ely on "Christ and Democracy"* might have been written by a Congregational Minister; and Canon Henson, in "Cross Bench Views of Church Questions," aims at partially congregationalising the Church of England. Yet neither of these writers take heed to the Congregational Church.

The Memorial Hall, situated as it is in the centre of London, close to Ludgate Circus, remains unnoticed by the thousands that hurry by. This Memorial Hall is the meeting-place of the Congregational Union of England and Wales, and of the London Congregational Union, and from this building the literature of the Church is issued by the Memorial Hall Publishing Company.

* "Christ and Democracy," by Charles W. Stubbs, D.D.

There are over 4,600 Congregational places of worship in England and Wales, containing over 400,000 Church members.* These numbers may not be very great, but the size and earnestness of some of the London congregations attest that the Church is gaining ground, and those who merely attend the Church services are in excess of actual Church Members, if we judge by statistics of Church sittings in England and Wales—an excess of over a million. The men of Mansfield College, Oxford, of which Dr. Fairbairn is the Principal, are quietly making their influence felt.

This Church sprang from the Separatists of the sixteenth century, when a small body of Puritans in the reign of Elizabeth gathered together as a free Church. They suffered bitter persecution, and the main strength of the movement was diverted to America, to

* See Congregational Year Book of England and Wales, 1902.

which most of them emigrated and there founded a colony—a colony which laid the foundation of the American Republic.

Before the close of the seventeenth century the Independents laid the corner-stone of British freedom, but in Great Britain their influence was more political than religious. Not so in America, where the religious influence of the Separatist emigrants is one of the most potent in the United States of to-day. The Free Churches there are mostly based on the broadest democratic lines of Church government, and the Congregational Church in the United States is in the vanguard of educational and missionary progress. If we consider the faith, reverence, and order which form the basis of these individualistic though democratic Churches, we shall catch a glimpse of those powers which tend to the stability of the great American Republic.

But we are now considering the development of these old Independent Churches in our own country.

The fundamental idea of Church government in the Congregational Church is, that the *People are the Church*. "Where two or three are gathered together in My name, there am I in the midst of them" (Matt. xviii. 20). All Church Members have an equal voice in matters of Church government, and in the election of the Minister of their Church, who is to be their Pastor and fellow-worker— to conduct their Church services, work amongst the poor, and to speak to them from the pulpit. The Minister claims no sacerdotal power. Deacons are elected to take charge of the finances of the Church and assist in the services.

The Church meetings of Members usually take place once a month for the consideration of matters connected with the Church, the Members of the

Church being people of all classes of the community, meeting on an equal footing as Christians, for mutual friendliness and support.

Each separate Independent Church elects its own Minister, and there is no central authority to manage the affairs of these Independent Churches as a whole. Dr. Parker's suggestion that there should be such an authority has perhaps not yet been fully discussed by the different Congregational assemblies.

I, however, do not wish to dwell on the difficult and complicated question of the details of Church government.

No human institution which exists is perfect, nor yet any form of government—all are open to some human imperfection. In secular life the democratic form of government seems to be now on trial, and not yet to have been found wanting so seriously as other forms of government have been found to be.

"The Fatherhood of God" and the "Brotherhood of Man" are fundamental Christian truths. The Church which founds its polity on these principles cannot be far from the truth—"Neither circumcision availeth anything, nor uncircumcision, but faith working through love" (Gal. v. 6).

All that is needed for inclusion in the Congregational Church, or perhaps, to be more accurate, for membership of one of these Independent Churches, is a statement as to "*Faith in Christ.*" Doctrinal definitions are not insisted on. I have before me the Church Manual of a West of London Congregational Church. "The Church admits candidates to its membership on their profession of faith in the Lord Jesus Christ, the Son of God, and Saviour of Mankind and their acceptance of His Will as the law, and His Spirit as the principle of their lives." Should their character, by flagrant misconduct, gainsay this simple confession of faith, they would be disfranchised from taking any part in Church government, but no one would interfere with them still joining in the services of the Church. The Church services are open to all, including the Communion service, and it would be left to a man's own conscience if, excluded from Church membership, he still wished to take part in the Communion service.

Any one wishing to join a Congregational Church would have a short conversation with some members of the congregation, and with the Minister, as to the earnestness of their faith. The Minister holds periodically a set of preparation classes for those considering Church membership, and for the children of Congregational parents arrived at an age to consider for themselves their Christian responsibility, and wishing to become communicants and Church Members. Those wishing to join this Church are not expected to define or dogmatically state their beliefs as to the "Incarnation," the "Atonement," or the "Redemption"; they are only expected to believe the spirit of these Christian doctrines. Their love of Divine Revelation, and the earnestness of their desire to live as followers of Christ, would be their credentials for membership. Dr. Parker has described the faith of this Church as "A Creedless, but potent and ever-enlarging faith."

Has not "Faith in Christ" in all Churches, of all times, and all various organisations and sects, been found to be "a potent and ever-enlarging Faith"? "Faith in Christ," as guide to conduct and endeavour, as strength in temptation, as hope in eternity, this would seem enough foundation to hold together a community of worshippers. This Church is sometimes called the "Disciples'" or "Learners'" Church. A Church for those who do not think that for them the Infinite can be defined in a few inches of print—in what is usually known as a "Creed." It is a Church for those who cannot feel that all religious questions were settled once and for ever by the ratification of the Church of England Prayer Book in 1517.

Although in the services of the Congregational Church the simplicity of Puritanism is retained, even the quietude of Quakerism, there is no *form of formlessness*. Reverence and simplicity are the keynotes of the Church. Where, however, the resources of the Church admit, much trouble is taken with the choir and music of the service.

In this Church baptism is believed to be an act of dedication to Christ. Infant baptism is usual. It is thought of as an act of dedication on the part of those who bring a child to be baptized, or, in the case of adult baptism, on the part of those who seek to be baptized themselves. It is not believed to have any regenerating power of itself, but it is a pledge that those who are baptized should seek to do the will of Christ.

The Ordinance of the Lord's Supper is believed to be a memorial and sign of our faith and calling as Christians. The Bread and Wine are administered to the Congregation by the deacons of the Church.

The Congregation remain seated. A short prayer by the Minister, and *silence*, a signing of our faith, solemn in its simplicity and meaning, far more solemn than the gorgeous ceremony of the Mass can make it. Suggesting no controversy, each soul may measure the significance of this symbolical act of faith and be thankful, according to its own immeasurable blessing.

This service is open to all who love Christ, whatever their denominational preferences may be.

There is no liturgy, no rigid form of

worship, in this Church. The prayers are extempory, as in the other Free Churches, and as they are in the Established Church of Scotland.

Though the service is non-political as a rule, the service is always in sympathy with the national feeling of the hour in which it is held. Chants from the Psalms and from the Prophetical books are sung, and there is usually an anthem. The hymn-book used in most London Congregational Churches is a beautiful collection of religious poetry, translations from the German, poems by Tennyson and Whittier, besides many of Wesley's hymns, and some of "Ancient and Modern." The simplicity of the service has none of the stiffness of the Presbyterian Church, or the extreme and crude Evangelical expression sometimes found in the other Free Churches, or in the Low Church of England service.

The preaching is broad in doctrine, deeply imbued with all the purest, most spiritual, and most human influences of modern thought and literature, accepting evolution, and some of modern Biblical criticism. Its Ministers are men of learning, with a courageous freedom of thought, but holding fast to the indestructible Gospel of Christ. We seem to have found that "Religion in unnoticed nooks has been weaving for herself new vestures,"* such as Carlyle dreamed of and failed to find in any visible Church of his day. This Church, as we have seen, true to its Puritanical traditions, knows no ritual observance, and its ceremonies are of the simplest. It has also retained simplicity in the architecture of its Church buildings and in interior decoration. That it sometimes adopts the façade of a Greek temple for the architecture of its churches may be an unconscious symbol— a symbol that it has discarded the Puritanism which strove against all re-

* Church Clothes, "Sartor Resartus," T. Carlyle.

ligious expression other than theological, either in Art, Literature, or Music, and which discountenanced every type of character except the ascetic. The Puritanism taught by this newer Church is the Puritanism of the spirit. It takes as a guide the early Christian teaching of a simple following of Christ, in all sincerity and simplicity of life, and it teaches us to take His life as a pattern. Self last, and all the manifold pursuits and interests of life but as a fulfilling of the doctrines of altruism and self-realisation, so that we, by our larger interests, should enrich the lives of others. If we seek to save our souls it should be that we may help the souls of others, not that we may coddle our own souls for our own comfort.

The papers which Professor Drummond read to the Free Church Theological Society, Glasgow, on "The New Evangelism" and "The Method of the New Theology," express the same spirit as is to be found in the present Congregational Church. In speaking of the Evangelical teaching of the past, he says, "Salvation was a thing that came into force at death," not a spiritual condition in the present as we now think of it; and he also says, "Religion was not so much a question of character as of status" ("The New Evangelism," p. 18).

"The New Evangelism" is, I think, expressed clearly in the following extract from a sermon preached by the Rev. C. S. Horne at the Kensington Chapel.

"Take again our modern conception of salvation. Here, too, it is perfectly true that when we speak of salvation we use the word in a different sense from the use made of it a generation back. But it is also true that we mean by it not less, but more. Salvation, in the old signification, was making sure of heaven. It had reference principally to life beyond the grave. It was the promise of eternity; and the question, 'Are you saved?' was used to mean 'Are you safe so far as eternity is concerned?' Now salvation means that still. But it means more than that. It covers time as well as eternity. It means the life that now is, as well as that which is to come. It means character purified, strengthened, sanctified. Moreover, the old term 'salvation' had, too frequently, reference only to that principle in man which was called spiritual. It did not mean the salvation of the whole man, mind and conscience and heart—yea, body, soul, and spirit. Yet that is what it means to-day. Salvation under the old ways of thinking dealt with a man as if he were a disembodied spirit. The mistake of failing to see the body for the spirit is almost as mischievous as the mistake of the materialist who fails to see the spirit for the body. We say to-day that unless a man present his body a living sacrifice, a pure temple, that man is not saved; nor can any orthodoxy of belief secure heaven for him, or him for heaven. Salvation is too great and majestic a term to be made merely the shibboleth of a school. We are trying to-day to rescue it from the cruelty and narrowness of its friends; from those who, in the spirit of the Athanasian Creed, are more anxious to refuse it to those who do not believe faithfully their definitions, than even to guarantee it to those who do. We aspire to make it less creedal than moral, and to guarantee it in God's name to all who come unto Him for life. The little belief cannot live. Men will not find food for faith in it. It is the enlarged faith that will live and that will win the belief of to-day and to-morrow. . . ." And, finally, take our modern conception of the Destiny of Mankind. I can hardly bring myself to refer to the belief general in the middle of this century that all the heathen who had never heard of Christ were lost for ever. Livingstone used to refer pathetically to the difficulty he felt in holding it in the face of the vast heathen populations. But not only so, every doctrine of an elect tended to the belief that only a very few would be snatched as salvage from the wreck of humanity. I do not pretend to say that the destiny of evil is clear to me. I feel such a horror of its power of resistance to light and love, that I dare not dogmatise in regard to its future, awful and mysterious as I feel it to be. But we have discovered to our shame that we have been ignoring all the sayings of the largest hope and most blessed promise. 'I, if I be lifted up, will draw all men unto Me.' 'God sent not His Son into the world to condemn the world, but that the world through Him might be saved.' These sayings, whatever they teach or do not teach, forbid the thought that the sublime issue of redemption is to be seen in the salvation of a mere handful of saints. That belief cannot live. It is too little. Only a great faith can live, for only a great faith is honouring to the great love of God."

A representative instance of Congregational preaching may also be found in the sermons of R. J. Campbell, of Brighton. His mysticism is somewhat influenced by Hegel. That creation is the result of a process in which the Deity realises Himself, "that in Christ God came to suffer with men, and also suffer for men. In the Cross of Christ we have something more than a symbol of the passion of Deity. In the suffering of Christ unknown depths are suggested. Without something that savours of irreverence we cannot penetrate far into the secret of that mysterious agony, we can but recognise that in the history of the Man of Sorrows a corner of the veil has been lifted, and we seem to discern something of that Divine Sorrow which lies behind and beneath the pain of humanity." *

Is not this "Creedless" Church perhaps

* "A Faith for Our Day," p. 223, R. J. Campbell.

after all gradually restating Christianity in terms which are understood by modern minds, in words that can be heard by modern ears? The Quaker standpoint of Silence on subjects of Infinitude, and Silence as a form of worship, is a wise, reverent, and deep-seeing standpoint. Silence on subjects too vast and deep for words or definition; but the Quakers could never be a proselytising Church, their Church could not become a Universal Church, but the Congregational Church, though not requiring dogmatic assertion from its Members, voices prayer and praise. And this omitting of definitions tends to unity of worship and to union of feeling of Christian people towards each other.

Mr. Balfour tells us (November 4, 1901), at the Glasgow Meeting on Church Extension, "He did not wholly conceal from himself the fact that there were at the present time special difficulties which the Church had got to contend with in dealing with those great religious problems; for it was impossible that religion should not be intertwined, and touch at many points, the general views and the general conception of the world and the history of the world in which they live. It must so teach it; and there had taken place a revolution during the last hundred years which he believed had no parallel in the recorded traditions of mankind. It was impossible that such a change as that should not carry with it the need and necessity, not of any change in Christian doctrine, but of a change in the *setting in which religion was from age to age presented to the people.*"

It is the "conventionalisation" of religion which dissatisfies many in the Church of England, and which prevents many from joining it. In considering those comparatively few, in the Church of England, who are restless and unsatisfied, what can be said to them in speaking of the Congregational Church appeals equally to those who are outside any Church, to the masses of our poor who are half puzzled, half repelled by the forms and dogmas of the Church of England, and by what seems to them as the wearisomeness and monotony of the Prayer-book service. The cry of the Evangelical Churches, as Mr. Asquith* truly said at Dr. Horton's anniversary gathering, is no longer "Save your soul," but "Save the souls of others."

This Congregational Church seems to succeed in expressing what the Broad Church of England has been striving to express, for "Broad Church" tendencies within the Church of England are not yet articulate. There are some in the Church of England who dream of a Church beyond; a Church that shall stand of itself, freed from formula, from special prescribed services for each day of the year, from prescribed fastings, freed

* See Report in *Times*, November, 1901.

from ritual on the one hand and from Puritanical narrowness and closely-defined doctrine on the other — freed from doctrines defined in words more expressive to former generations than to our own. Their wish also is for a Church in which individual interpretation reverently expressed shall have vent—they would find these strivings fulfilled in the Congregational Church. Recognising to the utmost that in the Church of England there are men, both priests and laymen, whose vision is as wide and whose religious fervour is as deep as that of any in the Congregational Church, still it seems obvious that the polity of the Congregational Church enables it to work with a freer spirit than is possible for the Established Church of England to work with at present. The Congregational Church can evolve a freer expression from within, and be open to freer influences from without.

In striving to meet the social needs of

to-day the Church of England is doing noble work—such work as is being done by many University Settlements and by the "Christian Social Union" is equivalent to the work being done by the Congregational Church. But if the Congregational Church has gained in spiritual things by its polity of brotherhood, it has also gained in power to cope with the needs of modern democracy, the Church itself being, as we have seen, intrinsically democratic in its constitution. "*The people are the Church*"—wherever and whenever two or three are gathered together in Christ's name, there is the Church.

The work that lies before the Churches is immense if they are at all to meet the growing needs of the concentrated population in our great towns, and to fight the ever-growing materialism which permeates all classes, from the highest to the lowest, in rural districts as well as in towns, for echoes of the town have reached the country. Dr. Horton's most interesting and valuable book lately published, "The Dissolution of Dissent," suggests the fusion of all Protestant Churches. It raises our hopes that the day may come when all Christian Churches shall realise their underlying Unity in Christ, and that together they may strive to unravel the tangled web of the many difficulties, spiritual, moral and social, which in these days are well nigh overwhelming in their complexity.

The Congregational Church in England is doing just such work as President Rooseveldt * in the *Fortnightly Review* of November, 1901, describes as being done by the Free Churches in America. "Every effort is made to keep in close touch with wageworkers, and this not merely for their benefit, but quite as much for the benefit of those who are kept in touch with them." Count Tolstoi, were he in England, would be a Con-

* "Reform through Social Work."

gregationalist. It is strange to read the story of his conversion, after his revolt from the dogmatism of the Greek Church in which he was reared, "No temple is needed; the true temple is the society of men united in love" ("The Spirit of Christ's Teaching," p. 4). Strange and of deep interest to read how this Titan of the North fought his battle with sin and darkness, doubt within his own heart, and corruption in the society in which he lived; how by the light of the Gospel, and of the inward guiding of the Spirit of God, he was guided to learn the Gospel of Christ *from* the poor—from the peasants that he lived amongst and whom he had in his earlier life been taught to despise (see "How I Came to believe," p 45).

In a recent publication of essays on vital subjects of our day, entitled "The Heart of the Empire," appears an essay by Charles Masterman. In dealing with the work of Social Settlements in the great centres of our population, he says, "When every Church is not only a place of Sunday worship, but also in its multifarious activities and offer of service a real settlement, then the admirers of Settlements can well reconcile themselves to see their own particular scheme merged in the wider ideal."

This wider ideal is already realised in the best Congregational Churches of to-day. Mr. F. W. Head, in an essay in the same volume on "The Church and the People," describes with great insight and power the way in which the Church of England should attack the problem of bringing spiritual help to the masses of poor in our great cities; and the methods he suggests are those of the Congregational Church, but of the existence of this Church he appears never to have heard.

If we face the problem of bringing spiritual enlightenment to our fellow-citizens who are without the Churches, and who discern but dimly the Kingdom of God, it is to this democratic Church alive to all pure-hearted human interests in politics, literature and art, that we should look for a great revival.

In the consecration and service to the poor insisted on by this Church, many of us may learn, as Tolstoi learnt, the gospel anew from the poor.

Not long ago some one described an active Congregational Church in the north-west of London as a Polytechnic Institution. The words were used casually and may appear flippant, but they express much. For a modern Congregational Church gathers round it manifold activities. All members of the Church, as such, are expected by their fellow-members to take some part either in the missionary or civilising work of the Church, if they have means and leisure to do so. Lectures on various branches of art are often delivered in the lecture-hall of the Church; a course of lectures on Wagner, illustrated by songs and instrumental music, or else a concert, may be given, various charitable meetings are held; and there are elocution, cooking and other classes. A debating club for young men assembles weekly, and a swimming and athletic club also exist in connection with the Church.

This Church may be commended to those who look for an Ethical Society permeated by Christian principles, and inspired by humanitarian enthusiasm for social service; to those too who, though they are working on secular lines, see the need for some spiritual guide among the mazes of problems that confront all who work among the poor in our great cities. For its teachings are intensely human. No emaciated asceticism here, but sacrifice for service. And no useless self-annihilation is enjoined: "This is the day of the Lord, let us rejoice and be glad in it," glad in work, and in enjoyment of all wholesome moderate recreations. It is a Church in close sympathy with the people, their economic needs and daily troubles; "Work-Worship"* might be its badge—Work for, and with, the poor. In fact the Congregational Church may be regarded as a microcosm of our best modern progressive activities; as a Renaissance of art and letters for the less leisured and poorer classes, joined to a fervent religious revival—a religious revival on simple undogmatic lines, an effort to make "Reason and the will of God prevail."

* "Aurora Leigh.'

A STUDY OF THE QUAKER IDEAL.

BY

WILLIAM EDWARD TURNER

(Recently Editor of "The British Friend.")

LONDON:

HEADLEY BROTHERS

14, BISHOPSGATE STREET WITHOUT, E.C.

1902.

Price Fourpence; 3s. 6d. per dozen.

"Happily, the bases of religion are few and solid. They teach men to look up to God as their Father, to Jesus as their Saviour, and to the Spirit of Him who sent His Son to save us, as the Source of Holiness and the Guide to Spiritual Truth. These are really the final and fundamental articles of Christianity."—
BISHOP FRASER.

"It is God's *Free Grace* that remits and blots out sin; of which the death of Christ and His sacrificing Himself was a most certain declaration and confirmation. This was not for the pacifying of God, but of man's conscience as to past sin."—WILLIAM PENN.

"Let nothing come between your souls and God but Christ."—GEORGE FOX.

A STUDY OF
THE QUAKER IDEAL.

INTRODUCTORY. The growth of human conceptions of moral and spiritual truth, like those of scientific knowledge, has been progressive. Little more than half a century has elapsed since most men believed as unquestioned truth that God created the world about 6,000 years ago in the space of six days. Now, how great is the change in the outlook on the distant ages, and the developments of the far-reaching centuries of the past. Science has taught us to look through a long antiquity at the slow but wondrous processes in the upbuilding of the physical structure of the world. Even the origin of man cannot be dogmatically limited to the period which used to be defined as the date of his appearance on the Earth.

Since men have come to comprehend more correctly, in the clearer knowledge that has been obtained, the conditions of at least some part of this vast universe, their thoughts of God have expanded, and the whole outlook on both natural and spiritual truth has been immensely widened. How much greater and grander is our new grasp of God's creative energy, and how surpassingly wonderful His handiwork appears. The orthodoxy of past centuries has harmonised some of the aspects of its theology with the clearer light which each century unfolds. The laws which govern the great processes of continuity are being better understood in every department of knowledge. Thoughtful men do not now look complacently on the dogma of the *un*-endingness of the physical torments of the lost, held so tenaciously in the middle ages, confirmed by the imagery of Milton in *Paradise Lost*, and even down to recent times. This distorted view is yielding to the illumination which has reached the conscience of many Christians by the teaching of the Spirit of Truth. The old idea is now felt to conflict with the loftier and purer conceptions of God's nature,—His love, His justice, His righteousness, and His Fatherhood. We can leave the unseen future to the " larger hope."

Many persons have felt in past days that religion, as it was often preached, tended to repress inquiry, and thus narrow the spiritual horizon. Many are seeking to-day something really catholic—of universal application ; a teaching which embraces and applies spiritual truth, whilst not at variance with natural law. This we believe the Quaker Ideal of Christ's Christianity meets.

WITNESS OF TRUTH. Let us then turn our thoughts to some aspects of spiritual truth, as they are presented in the light of the teaching of our Lord. We are familiar with the incidents narrated by the apostle John, which formed a part in the process of that great drama of the world's history, when the divine Carpenter of Nazareth stood arraigned by the authorities of His own nation,—the Chief Priests, Pharisees and Scribes —before the representative of Imperial Rome. The question which Pilate put to Jesus in the bewilderment of his perplexed thoughts, was a natural one. It has been raised in many a human soul in each succeeding generation. Are there not anxious and sincere hearts asking that question to-day?—though nineteen centuries have rolled their course since Christ so nobly yet so simply declared to Pilate, "To this end was I born, and to this end am I come into the world, that I should bear witness unto the Truth. Every one that is of the truth" (—loveth or seeketh truth—) "heareth my voice."

Such words lead us to two considerations. What is the nature of the Teacher who advanced such claims, and made such demands on the attention of mankind? And what is the nature of the Race to whom it would be possible to address such a momentous issue as the last sentence involves? Long ago the Hebrew Psalmist had asked the question, "What is man that thou art mindful of him, or the son of man that thou visiteth him? Thou hast made him but a little lower than God. Thou has crowned him with glory and honour." (R.V.)

Man is not a mere machine, set a-going by a skilled contriver, and left to work out the issues of life by mechanical processes. He possesses a dual nature. His physical organism is a marvellous production of creative power, by whatever far-off processes of infinite wisdom his Maker was pleased to perfect his wonderful structure, and adapt the human habitation for the reception of that heaven-born inspiration, that inbreathing of a spiritual nature, by which God has made him a living soul capable of receiving the impress of His own divinity.

This spiritual capacity, however infantile its incipient life and power may have been, is the ground for the reception of all the moral and spiritual training of his history. It is the faculty by which light, knowledge, and understanding enter into his being, form his character, mould his nature, and manifest his will.

The late Professor Fiske, in his book on "Man's Destiny," suggests the thought that God, having evolved the wondrous human organism, developed the faculty of reason and intelligence, and perfected the material side of man's being, is now evolving the spiritual destiny of the race, and leading the soul,— that inner consciousness which He has quickened by the breath of His own spirit,—to fuller and more perfect reception of His divine nature, until there shall be known, as now by the individual, so by the race, the far-off yet ever approaching realisation of the Eternal Life. This Life was perfectly manifested once in the human life of Jesus Christ, of whom the Apostle Paul writes, "In Him dwelt the fulness of the Godhead bodily."

MAN'S DUAL NATURE. It is important that we intelligently recognise the truth, or as we may say, the facts concerning man's dual nature. Universal experience confirms the truth that the lower or earthward side of our being ever seeks those things which please and gratify the flesh; we are so familiar with the wilful and wayward tendencies of our natural man,—so sorrowfully acquainted with self-rule which begets sin, that none of us need to be reminded that *we* have indeed sinned, and like all our brothers come short of the glory—or purpose- of God. Nor are we ignorant of the fact that there comes to our spiritual nature an influence—other than of self—a Power that makes for righteousness, a soundless Voice that reproves for wrong and evil, and woos to goodness and truth,—this is the Voice of the Spirit of God.

The history of the Jewish nation, through whom the clearest spiritual teaching has come to mankind, is a history of a progressive revelation of God, and of truth. Neither Abraham, nor Moses, nor Elijah, nor the divinely taught Isaiah, saw the fulness of God's nature, or realised more than a partial knowledge of His character and will. But God was always teaching, as He still teaches, both by good and evil, by failure and success. Through His dealings in providence, as well as by the inspired utterances of His prophets, He was opening out the knowledge of His will as men were able to apprehend it. He has been ever working by the hidden operations of His grace on the heart, bringing conviction and condemnation for evil, assuring the wrong-doer of pardon, whenever it was honestly sought, and stimulating into better ways and a higher life. It has been very aptly said, I think by the late Canon Liddon, that "Truth is not manifested once for all, but by slow and gradual processes divinely controlled: much is seen through a glass dimly, but is ever unfolding in a divine evolution, and marching onward to far-off good."

It is not that truth can ever change, or that God can be of one character yesterday and another to-day. God and truth are alike unchangeable, and the revelation of truth to the soul has ever depended and must ever depend on conditions of receptivity, as well as on those of intellectual and spiritual environment which are but partially under his control.

CHRIST'S HUMANITY AND DIVINITY.

When the Divine Babe was born in Bethlehem, the Giver of life and light made to our race such a revealing of Himself and of spiritual truth as the world had never known, and which, though centuries have intervened, men have yet but in part apprehended. Wherever that apprehension has been the clearest, and men have had the truest vision of God, it has been in those souls who, like John, have leaned on the bosom of the World's Redeemer, have drunk of His spirit of grace and love, and received the new nature of Divine self-abnegation, which permeated and sanctified that human life. The birth of Christianity may truly be said to be the dawn of a new era in the spiritual evolution of the race. The Christ who came, at once God's messenger and His message, in whom the light of the knowledge of the glory (or purpose) of God has been revealed, has brought to men such an unveiling of their Father's face as can alone answer the ceaseless craving of their spiritual nature, and bring them satisfying rest. We may not be able to demonstrate the conditions under which He came, and by which He went, but the sincere mind cannot fail to be conscious of an intuitive conviction, an inward witness of the truth that the Christ who lived and taught on the hilly slopes of Galilee, on the shores of Gennesaret, in the synagogues of Capernaum and Nazareth, in the streets and in the temple of Jerusalem, stands out UNIQUE among the Race. He claims a position and assumes a character which none before or since have ever dared to take; and whether as Son of God or Son of man, He manifests by the whole tenor of His life the wondrous truth of His words, "I and the Father are one" (John x. 30).

Let us attempt for a few moments to reflect on the chief characteristics of the Messiah. The character of Christ must of necessity be the essence of Christianity. No less is it true that Christianity is bound up in the essential character of Christ. What then is the chief feature of His life, and what the nature of His teaching? He who claims to be the Son of God, one with God, whom He calls His Father, lives a human life; He is made like unto His brethren, the world of humanity; He enters the earthly environment under conditions that are incident to the race. We learn that He was tempted in all points like others are tempted, that He hungered and thirsted, that He passed through the conflict between good and evil, but never yielded in the fight; He sorrowed and grieved, sympathised and loved, and wept human tears; His sufferings were sharp indeed, nay, so keen were they in the bitter sense of the world's blight of sin and weight of woe, that they broke His tender heart. But what differentiated Him from His fellows? His consciousness of a Divine origin was ever present with

Him all through that short but eventful life. It was with Him in every stage of that momentous career, from those years of early childhood when His parents sought the absent child, and remonstrated with their boy, who had been talking with the doctors in the temple and amazing them with His answers, calmly replying, "Wist ye not that I must be about My Father's business?"—with Him even under the cloud of the sad lone hour whilst suffering the agony of Gethsemane and then of the Cross;—with Him when He commended His Spirit into the hands of His Father, and prayed for those who placed Him there, saying, "Father, forgive them, they know not what they do."

Through all the course of that dedicated life it had been "his meat and drink to do the will of the Father who had sent Him." In Him dwelt the Father's spirit perfectly, and by His spirit He perfectly fulfilled the Father's will. He not only taught the truth about God, but the evidence of that truth was His own life. And because His life was in perfect accord with the will of God throughout all its eventful conditions, we can thankfully recognise His claim as "Son of God," and crown Him "King of men."

CHRIST'S REVELATION. Let us turn to the nature of His teaching. He had proclaimed Himself a King; what was the nature of His Kingdom? He declared that it was a heavenly Kingdom, a Kingdom of righteousness and truth not built up by, though in the midst of, human conditions, nor yet established by the ambitions of human power. Riches, honour, might, statecraft, diplomacy, expediency; these had no name in His Kingdom. LOVE is the primal motto that shines in living light over the gateway into the Kingdom which He sets up, and over which He reigns. And He does not hesitate to tell a world embittered by the hatreds, jealousies and malice of its self-governed and evil heart,—and which yet, below its unrest, is longing for deliverance from itself,—that the God He proclaims is ETERNAL LOVE, that He is no other, and no less, than *their* FATHER, as He is His *own* FATHER, and that He has come because that Father so loved them that He had sent Him to bring them the utmost assurance of that love. He came to redeem men from sin, with all its dire result; from self, which is apartness from God, and so to fill them with the spirit of sonship, that they might learn to cry with him, "Abba Father," and know His spirit to bear witness within them that they were ordained to this blessed inheritance. Whittier in his poem on *Revelation* says:—

> I know He is, and what He is,
>   Whose one great purpose is the good
> Of all. I rest my soul on His
>   Immortal Love and Fatherhood;
>   And trust Him, as His children should.

Ian Maclaren (Dr. John Watson), makes the following statement in his *Mind of the Master*. He says that "Jesus cast his whole doctrine of sin into the drama of the Prodigal Son, and commands our adherence by its fidelity to life. The parable moves between the two poles of ideal and real human life; home, where the sons of God live in moral harmony with their Father, which is liberty; and exile, where they live in riotous disobedience, which is licence. He fixes on his representative sinner, and traces his career with great care, and various subtle touches. His father does not compel him to stay at home; he has free will. The son claims his portion; he has individuality. He flings himself out of his father's house; he makes a mischoice. He plays the fool in the far country; this is the fulfilling of his bent. He is sent out to feed swine; this is the punishment of sin. He awakes to a bitter contrast; this is repentance. He returns to obedience; this is salvation. Salvation—which is spiritual health—is the restoration of spiritual order, the close of the bitter experience. . . . Heaven, according to Jesus, was to be with God in our Father's house; hell was to be away from God, in the far country. Each man carried his heaven in his heart, 'the Kingdom is within you'; or his hell in a gnawing remorse, and heat of lust, 'where their worm dieth not and the fire is not quenched.'" Again he writes :—"Jesus proposed to ransom the race, not by paying a price to the devil or to God, but by loosening the grip of sin on the heart and re-enforcing the will. He would redeem *us*. The service of His life and the sacrifice of His death would infuse a new spirit into humanity, and be its regeneration. 'The Son of man came not to be ministered unto, but to minister, and to give His life a ransom for many.'" It has been well said by another modern writer :—"Christ brought into the world a spiritual life which transforms humanity by regenerating its inner spirit."

MAN'S NEED OF RECONCILIATION. Man has ever felt the need of a soul-satisfying way of approaching and trusting God. Soul hunger has been universally, though often blindly expressed. "Oh that I knew where I might find Him" is still the cry of humanity. God has met this need by the gift of His Son, in whom we receive the most satisfying consciousness of at-one-ment. — "God was, in Christ, reconciling the world unto Himself, not reckoning unto them their trespasses." His ministers proclaim this word of reconciliation. "We are ambassadors, therefore, on behalf of Christ; we beseech you, be *ye* reconciled to God." God was, and is always on our side. He hates sin, but loves and yearns over the sinner. Christ "gave Himself for us, the just on behalf of the unjust, that He might bring *us to God.*" The days are happily declining when men closed the gates of the heavenly kingdom against all who do not pass the portals by the same limited beliefs by which they themselves have entered.

For myself, I am thankful to rest on the deep conviction,—after a careful study of the spirit of our Lord's teaching,—that the Sacrifice of the Cross was not a mere judicial transaction between Jesus and God to purchase God's favour, to alter or change God's purpose for the race; but was rather the revelation and seal of an antecedent and eternal love, a pledge in the new covenant, by His incarnation and death, of the free bestowal of pardoning grace to a truly penitent soul; assuring him of welcome to that Father's heart, Who is ever seeking his return, and ever waiting to forgive and to restore. Surely in this, for man, is "the Reconciliation of the Cross."

THE DIVINE FATHERHOOD. The divine Fatherhood was as dear in Jesus for the race, as for Himself; and He testifies of it as lying at the foundation of all truth He had come to bear witness to. This primary fact was not new, though but dimly perceived even by the choicest spirits of the chosen people. But from the lips of Christ it comes, a fresh revelation to weary and burdened hearts, and brings hope and comfort to the outcast and heavy laden. To be told that men are God's children, and shall know it, if they will but open their heart to the breath of heaven and the quickening grace of the spirit of love ;—that God intends them to be brothers in the great family of their Father's house ;—that He comes to deliver them from the thraldom of sin which is the bondage of self, and lift them into a *new life,* in which His spirit shall be their helper, their counsellor, their comforter, and their guide ;—this is indeed glad tidings of great joy, the echoes of which reverberate all down the Christian ages and should fall upon our ears, and enter into the depths of our souls afresh to-day with a wealth of hope and grace, that grows wider and fuller as the centuries advance. To be assured of the great truth that a purpose of love runs all along the tangled course of human life, seeking with open arms to gather the wanderer, and rescue the perishing, to pardon the sin-stained and forgive the erring, to bind up the broken hearted, give deliverance to the moral captive, sight to the spiritually blind and hearing to the deaf : to make men strong for the duty and service of life, and brace them to victory in the conflict with evil by a grace and power *not their own*, but freely given in Jesus Christ;—surely this is a gospel of truth,—a gospel for all sorts and conditions of men.

THE DYNAMIC FORCE OF CHRISTIANITY. It has been often said that the dynamic force of a Religion is devotion to a person. The dynamic force of Christianity lies in devotion to Christ. By that devotion men have followed the footsteps of their Master, and won His victories with Him. The noblest souls that have lived and wrought in the Christian ages have been moved by the ceaseless energy of that living spirit which dwelt in Him without stint or measure, and by which He draws men to Himself that He may impart to them His mind, and the self-sacrificing devotion to truth and goodness from which He never swerved. "And I, if I be lifted up from the earth, will draw all men unto myself."

What part then have *we* in the spirit of devotion and of faithful loyalty to the despised Nazarene? Has the world more attraction for us than He has who overcome it? Have things of time and sense more hold on our affections, our aims and energies, than the things of His Kingdom which is not of this world and which will not pass away? In short, have we any part in the experience of the Apostle Paul, who, though not lacking in force of intellect, or strength of character, or opportunity for the aggrandisement of self, turned right round in his course, and became obedient to the heavenly vision. It was through this obedience he reached the experience which made him able to write, " I am crucified with Christ, nevertheless I live, yet no longer I, but Christ liveth in me, and the life which I now live in the flesh, I live in faith, the faith which is in the Son of God, who loved *me*, and gave himself for *me*."

Let us think of those noble lines of Whittier, in his poem on *Requirement*, so simple, yet so full of truth :—

> " We live by Faith ; but Faith is not the slave
> Of text and legend.   Reason's voice and God's,
> Nature's and Duty's, never are at odds.
> What asks our Father of His children, save
> Justice, and mercy, and humility,
> A reasonable service of good deeds,
> Pure living, tenderness to human needs,
> Reverence and trust, and prayer for light to see
> The Master's footprints in our daily ways ?
> No knotted scourge, nor sacrificial knife,
> But the calm beauty of an ordered life
> Whose very breathing is unworded praise !—
> A life that stands as all true lives have stood,
> Firm-rooted in the faith that God is Good."

The gospel which Christ preached was not an attempt to invent new doctrines or discover new truths. The great aim of His teaching was to *un*cover truth and invest it with *reality*. He proved that reality by His own life, and appealed to a witness in each human breast to verify its righteousness. It is true He made such a revolution from the teaching of His day, that while the common people heard Him gladly, their teachers—the doctors of divinity,—the subtle scribes,—the hypocritical Pharisees—stood aghast at His utterances, for they swept the ground on which Priest and ritual alike stood. No wonder they sought to compass His death. Christ opened His wonderful exposition of God's truth by blessing the very conditions which Rabbis had despised and cast out. The poor in spirit are to possess the Kingdom, the pure in heart are to see God,—the mourners, the meek, the merciful, the peacemakers, the hungry and thirsty souls panting after better things, the faithful ones persecuted for goodness sake,—these are the children of His kingdom, the salt of the earth, the lights of the world, the city set upon a hill. Men instinctively feel that such souls have a heaven-born possession, and the attractive force of their lives becomes an ever increasing force in the world, redeeming men from its sinful lusts, its false and hollow pretences, its love of greed and gain, its worship of self. Christ tells of a spirit that is like the wind which blows whence it listeth, but which comes with quickening energy and changes the old and earthly nature, not by removing it, but by subduing it, and bringing it into complete control to a higher order of life. What more natural then, but that, as Christ preached *reality* and not profession,—so *character* rather than beliefs should be the great object He seeks to impress.

APPLICATION OF PRINCIPLE TO WORSHIP. The principle that "the Kingdom of God is not in word but in power," should be applied to all branches of Christian life and service, and enter into all worship of the Supreme. Christ uttered no formula of conditions for the conduct of public worship. He taught men that "God is a Spirit,"—and that "they that worship Him, must worship in spirit and in truth." He told them the Father seeks such worship from them; and He left them the unspeakably blessed legacy of His spirit to guide into such adaptation of conditions as should most perfectly aid the intelligent worship of the *heart*. This duty has been universally recognised by Christians meeting together to offer unitedly homage to God their common Father. The methods applied for mutual help and edification in their worship are very varied. With a large body of Christians a prescribed liturgy is used as worship, with a system of ritual, more or less complex, administered by a separated class, usually called priests, both in the Anglican and in the Roman profession. In what may be described as the Nonconformist or Free Churches, a simpler order obtains; a minister being set apart to lead the congregation in song and prayer, to read the Scriptures, and to deliver a discourse prepared or otherwise, according to a settled order of service. In each of these systems the appointed conductor of public worship usually passes through a special education and college training to fit him for the office, and is salaried for the fulfilment of the duties he undertakes. He becomes the indispensable leader of the service of the congregation, without whose presence and guidance public worship would cease, or by whose absence it would be seriously crippled. This system, though so widely adopted, opens a door to spiritual dependance on professional aids in public worship; yet it has had a vast influence for good on a large proportion of its adherents. The salaried ministry, whether in a State Established Church or in Free Churches, has done and is doing a noble work for all classes of the community. Many of those so engaged are inspired men; they are instructors of the ignorant and winners of souls; they honour their office.

We are inquiring now, not of the relative excellence of the several systems in general use, but we are inquiring as to what method in worship brings us into closest relation to truth and reality, and into spiritual communion with God.

It is a generally recognised fact that there are many thoughtful people who are somewhat weary of formal services, however imposing the ritual, or artistic the rendering of music and song. They often feel a sense of *un*reality lying beneath a sensuous exterior of sound, and a ceremonial performance of routine utterance. They are seeking for a more soul-satisfying, a freer and simpler approach to God.

Let me therefore attempt to describe another method which is perhaps unique—though by no means perfect—in the simplicity of its arrangements, and the spirituality of its ideals in public worship. It represents an order of things which is based on the primary principles enunciated by Christ, "God is a Spirit; and they that worship Him must worship in spirit and in truth." These words evidently indicate that what is offered as homage to God, must be consciously felt, and be the true and sincere oblation of the heart. To reach such an experience of Christ's presence and power, the seeker after truth will strive to attain.

It is to such a realisation of Christ's unseen but living Presence the congregations of the Religious Society of Friends (Quakers) seek to gather. They have no minister or priest set apart to conduct their service, no mediator whose offices come between their souls and the invisible Teacher, whose spiritual Presence is sought, and Who has promised to meet with all who gather in His name. Their basis is a common brotherhood; they assemble in silence, without a previously planned vocal service. Vocal utterances are frequent, but are not essential in their worship. Words of prayer and exhortation may be expressed by any who believe the Holy Spirit gives them a message for the people. The service of ministry rendered by their members is offered freely; their religious work is voluntary.

In their worship they seek to realise the presence of the great Over-soul, who filleth all space, to Whom all conditions are as an open book, Who reads both the thought and intent of the heart, and Who, by the direct influence of His spirit, can alone beget real homage and worship. They gather in stillness, not as an end, but as, in their view, the best means to reach the truest result. That end is, to become, through sincere heart effort, conscious recipients of a divine uplifting,—inwardly quickening a fresh sense of dependance on, and gratitude to God for all spiritual good and blessing. Spoken or unspoken prayer becomes the expression of a real soul-hunger for the grace which comes from God Himself, through direct, and not proxical, contact with Christ's spiritual presence. This is the communion of the bread of life. Whilst they disclaim any monopoly of the Holy Spirit, they regard His influence as an indispensable factor in true worship. The personal realisation of this experience becomes their first object. Hence they sit down in silence, without the aid of music and song, or any sensuous accompaniment, to hold united communion with the Father of spirits, and to listen to His still small Voice, bringing conviction to the heart for wrong in thought or deed, and a sense of forgiveness wherever it is honestly sought, freely offered in Jesus Christ. By this inward quickening, which comes through contact with the divine Redeemer, He imparts renewal of strength for the right fulfilment of the manifold duties of life; gives comfort to the troubled and afflicted;—peace and rest to the burdened and heayy laden;—and inspires the hope that reaches out beyond all visible conditions to the full fruition of faith, when the faltering service of earth shall be completed, and

> "Heaven shall make perfect
> Our *im*perfect life."

Whilst they have a keen enjoyment of music and song in social life, and believe they may be elevating to the mind, as well as artistically pleasing,—they fear that the introduction into public worship of a stated service of song, accompanied by a choir and instrumental music, has frequently the tendency to diminish the *personal* effort of a truly spiritual and *inwardly realised* worship; and naturally leads the mind off from the highest conception of divine fellowship, to lower and inferior objects of desire. They believe that spontaneity, rather than formality of service, conduces to a fuller realisation of the divine presence and power. Hence they desire that all vocal offering of ministry or prayer in worship should be made under a direct sense of the guidance and impulse of the Spirit of Christ, in whose name and to whose presence all must come who would worship God as He has taught us.

It is instructive and interesting to observe how this subject impressed the mind of no less an authority than the Archbishop of York. When delivering his Address at a meeting of the Convocation of the Northern Provinces, held in York Minster, in 1899, he emphasises the value and need of silence in worship in the following statement. He said "that he had been impressed with that feature in the service of the people called 'Friends,' which consisted in spending a considerable time in absolute silence, often, indeed, continuing through the whole service. For years he had been under the impression that churchmen underrated the blessing and the necessity for silence in public worship. It is true that people sometimes made that feature in the service of 'Friends,' a subject for criticism, and almost for merriment, and said that they sat still and sometimes went back to their homes without anything having been said. The fact was that having waited upon God in silence, they had done a very great deal, and might possibly have received a greater blessing than if they had been occupying the time in uttering their own words addressed to God, or in other acts of worship. It had long been his desire to introduce this feature, where possible, into the service of the Church of England."

Another writer (Maeterlinck) much impressed by the need of greater simplicity and inwardness in present day religion, and in public worship, says:—
"It is well for bodies of men to group themselves into gatherings for the observance of silence, for by that attitude of mind alone can the reverent frame be attained by which the soul can commune directly with its Maker." Surely such testimonies may well lead us to commend to other thoughtful Christians an experience so eminently helpful to the growth and stability of the spiritual life.

THE PRINCIPLE IN RELATION TO ORDINANCES. The realisation of the divine inwardness of the teaching of Jesus, both by parable and metaphor, lies at the basis of the Quaker Ideal in reference to what are called "The Ordinances." They accept Christ's utterances on Baptism and on the Supper in the light of their spiritual significance as that which alone constitutes their force and reality in the experience of true Christian life and service. The Baptism of Christ is a heart renewing and inwardly purifying work of His spirit. No external symbol can ever take its place, but may even be dangerously substituted for the reality by superficial minds trusting in a rite, and expecting from it sacramental grace.

In like manner the true Supper becomes no longer a typical sign of an inward grace, but is the Christian's constant participation of the body and blood of Christ, by virtue of the soul-quickening and sustaining energy of His abiding Presence; it is He who nourishes the spiritual life day by day, vitalising its springs of service and faith, and producing in His followers the genuinely realised experience of His own words:—"He that eateth my flesh and drinketh my blood abideth in Me, and I in him. As the living Father hath sent Me, and I live because of the Father; so he that eateth Me, he also shall live because of Me." And again:—"It is the spirit that quickeneth, the flesh (that which is merely visible and external) profiteth nothing. The words that I have spoken unto you are spirit and are life."

They who, in the spirit of the Master, thus grasp and appropriate the inwardness of His teaching will feel that they are no longer dependent on symbol or type, on priest or altar. Unlike those who served in the symbol worship of a former dispensation, whose ordinances the apostle Paul reminds us "could not make the comers thereunto perfect as pertaining to the conscience," the disciple of Jesus under the new covenant has passed from the shadow and come to the substance itself; to the "GRACE and TRUTH which came by Jesus Christ," who in His abiding Presence is Head over all things in His church, High Priest—alone and for ever—over the house of God.

How truly do the words of Tennyson emphasise the thought we seek to impress:

> "Our human systems have their day,
>   They have their day and cease to be;
>   They are but broken lights of Thee,
> And THOU, O Lord, art more than they."

In a recent publication (1901) on *Christian Ordinances and Social Progress*, Freemantle, the Bishop of Ripon, frankly and courageously says:—"We may be thankful that there is a body of Christians, distinguished for their Christian simplicity and good works, who have altogether discarded the use of outward sacraments. To deny them the Christian name and a place in the Christian Church would be to deny the Spirit of God. The 'Friends' stand as a witness that the body of believers has complete power over the outward form."

The apostle John, who gives such a graphic record of the last utterances and commands of our Lord, and who was in such close touch with the Master he loved as he sat at the last supper Christ ate with his disciples, leaves no suggestion that the Lord intended to institute a sacramental rite. Such an obligation would have been altogether at variance with the spirituality and inwardness of all His teaching. The divine energy of Christ, operating within the sphere of the individual soul, is the divine element in producing the new life, and in sustaining its vitality through all the stages of its development to the fulness of the stature of the perfect man in Christ.

CONCLUSION. These primary conceptions of truth, going back to the fountain of spiritual life, may be said to represent the main features of the Quaker Ideal, and to differentiate the profession of Christianity held by the Society of Friends. They make no exclusive claim to be the only interpreters of truth,—they hold no monopoly of the Gospel, no spiritual possession that is not the inheritance of every human brother. They claim no infallibility from human misapprehensions, but they seek to go behind the creeds and formularies that have grown with the ages, to touch the spiritual garment of Christ's Presence, and read the lessons that fell from His lips. They have nothing to add to the primal truth He taught concerning God and concerning man; but would rather seek to remove the accretions of theological schools and systems, and diminish impediments to the progress of light and knowledge. Modern Biblical Research is leading men back to simpler and clearer conceptions of truth, for which we may be devoutly thankful. The result of these critical inquiries and of the careful analyses of Scripture records, has not been to dethrone Christ, or to destroy, or even lessen His witness to the truth; but rather to lift Him higher than ever, and to give men yet nobler conceptions of the character and attributes of God. Quakerism believes that the Gospel of Jesus is a living message to every generation of our Race. It appeals neither to Priest or Sacrament, but invites to direct fellowship with Christ as an Eternal Presence, Who is ever leading men onward and upward to the perfect light and love, of God. Let us cherish the hope anticipated by Whittier, when he writes :

> " The world sits at the feet of Christ,
>   Unknowing, blind, and unconsoled ;
>   It yet shall touch His garment's fold,
> And feel the heavenly Alchemist
>   Transform its very dust to gold."